A583

JOP

EATING OUT ORIENTAL

LORI OHLIGER

DAVID & CHARLES
Newton Abbot   London

B.I. PUBLICATIONS
Bombay   Calcutta   Madras   New Dehli

British Library Cataloguing in Publication Data

Ohliger, Lori
  Eating out oriental.
  1. Cookery, Oriental – Terminology
  2. Restaurants, lunch rooms, etc.
  I. Title
  641.595   TX724.5.A1

  ISBN 0-7153-8345-0

Typeset by Typesetters (Birmingham) Limited
Smethwick, Warley, West Midlands
and printed in Great Britain
by Redwood Burn Limited, Trowbridge, Wilts
for David & Charles (Publishers) Limited
Brunel House Newton Abbot Devon

CONTENTS

HOW TO USE THE GLOSSARY

This glossary is designed to help the occidental diner enjoy oriental dining by listing in alphabetical order, separated by country, short descriptions of foods he or she may encounter in oriental restaurants in the UK, US or abroad (wherever menu items are listed in the Roman alphabet). The glossary is not an all-comprehensive guide; it is impossible to list all the dishes one may confront on a menu. On the other hand, a dish may be listed in the glossary more than once but under another name because there is no one uniform system for transliterating oriental languages into the Roman alphabet; and also because one dish may have many different names. Thus, it is hoped the diner will find a dish listed even though it is spelt or referred to in more than one manner. At the end of the main section on each country is a list of useful words, generally ingredients or sauces.

The countries covered in the glossary include: China, India, Japan, Korea, Indonesia, Malaysia/Singapore, Thailand, Vietnam and the Philippines. Although it would have been desirable to divide space equally among the countries represented, common sense and practical considerations have ruled against this. Even so, we hope diners will be equally helped to enjoy their food in a Vietnamese or a Chinese restaurant, having selected it with the help of the glossary.

CHINA

Ba bao fan; baat bo faahn Steamed glutinous rice pudding decorated with preserved fruits and jam.

Ba bao op Duck stuffed with ham, Chinese sausage, dried shrimp, peanuts, bamboo shoots and glutinous rice flavoured with ginger.

Ba bao yang ping go Steamed fruit-nut mixture.

Ba bao yu Literally 'eight treasure duck' – boned duck stuffed with rice, pork, shrimps, mushrooms, water chestnuts, gingko nuts, chestnuts, bamboo shoots and roasted.

Ba tsu tu dou Fried potato fritters served in heated sweet syrup.

Baak faahn yu; bai fan yu Herring fillets in batter with egg yolk cover on one side and egg white cover on the other.

Baak fahn Boiled rice.

Baak jaahm ghuy; bai tsan ji Chicken boiled with wine, rubbed with sesame seed oil, cut into bite-size pieces and served with a simple sesame seed oil sauce.

Baau yuh wuih seung dung Abalone slices quick-simmered in sauce of red-cooked pork (pork simmered in soy-based broth) and served with winter mushrooms and bamboo shoots to lend texture contrast.

Bai chieh ro Boiled pork sliced and served with a sauce of soy, vinegar, sesame oil, ginger, scallions and red peppers.

Bai dzan gee Boiled chicken cut into bite-size pieces and served garnished with ham and sauce of oyster sauce and hot mustard.

Bai go gee chiu Breast of chicken boned and stir-fried with snow peas, mushrooms and gingko nuts.

Bai jr zo sun Boiled bamboo shoots covered in a soy-based sauce and garnished with minced ham.

Bai shueh gee Mixture of minced meats – chicken breast, shrimp, fish fillet and pork, bound with egg white and quick-fried; served with a garnish of chopped ham and scallions.

Bai tzahn gee Boiled chicken with ginger, soy and oyster sauce.

Bai tze yo yu Dried squid reconstituted and cooked in a white sauce of thickened chicken stock garnished with Chinese mushrooms and Chinese cabbage hearts and ham.

Ban kwai yu Canned salmon salad dressed with ginger, scallions and sesame oil.

Ban san si Salad of kohlrabi, shredded celery cabbage, flavoured with anise, peppers and sesame oil.

Ban yah Steamed duck hung in the sun to remove moisture, usually referred to as pressed duck.

Bao yu bai tsai shing Abalone slices with Chinese cabbage hearts and oyster sauce.

Bao yu ju gee mun yu tse Cornish hens steamed and boned flavoured with scallions, ginger and sherry garnished with shark fins, mushrooms and abalone.

Bao yu pien Cold abalone slices served with a simple sauce of abalone liquid and soy.

5

Bark cheuk har Poached shrimps served with a sauce of garlic, onion, chilli peppers and soy.

Bark fa yeung high kim Crab claws stuffed with shrimp and pork mixture and deep-fried.

Bart jun dow foo hung Soup of meat, vegetables and bean curd.

Bart jun dung gua lup tang; ba jen dung gua la tang Winter melon, vegetables and pork or chicken slices in a clear broth.

Bat su ping guo Apple slices cooked in sugar syrup and dipped in cold water prior to eating to harden sugar coating.

Bau haahm yuh siu yuhk Pork belly simmered in mixture of soy, water, sugar and wine and flavoured with salted fish served with abalone slices.

Bau yu dung goo; bao yu dung gu Cold abalone slices and mushrooms in a mild soy-sherry sauce.

Baw law ghuy Chicken braised with pineapple covered with a sauce of soy, garlic and sesame oil.

Baw law gnaap Slices of roast duck dressed with mustard, sesame seeds and vinegar, served garnished with pineapple slices and onion rings.

Bei jing kao ya; jia ting Peking ya 'Peking duck'—duck smeared with honey and spices, roasted until the skin is crispy and can be separated from the body as it is considered a delicacy and is eaten separately rolled in thin pancakes with spring onions and hoisin sauce. The meat of the duck is sliced in bite-size pieces and is eaten with its own sauce.

Bi yu shan hu 'Green jade and red coral'—crab eggs fried with the stems of green vegetables.

Bi yur twei pien Stir-fried mixture of snow peas, ham, Chinese mushrooms and bamboo shoots flavoured with ginger.

Bing tong gee Chicken legs and wings marinated in soy and sherry stir-fried with black mushrooms and bamboo shoots, flavoured with rock sugar and scallions.

Bing tong huhk yih; ring tang mu er White wood ears (a chewy, fleshy fungus) simmered in a broth of sugar and water making a simple, light ending to a rich meal.

Bo lo bon shu op Boned roast duck served with a sauce of peanut butter, vinegar, sugar and pineapple juice.

Bo lo gai Stir-fried chicken pieces flavoured with ginger slices and pineapple chunks and juice, served with celery and carrot slices.

Bo lo lychee gai kew Boned breast of chicken cubes deep-fried and served with a sweet-sour sauce garnished with litchi nuts, cherries and pineapples.

Bo lo niu ro Beef stir-fried with ginger and scallions served with pineapple pieces and garnished with almonds.

Bo lo op Bite-size pieces of duck boiled in pineapple juice and served in a sauce of ginger, sherry and soy garnished with celery, carrots and pineapple chunks.

Bo lo ying to tseng go Steamed pineapple-cherry pudding.

Bo lo yoke Stir-fried pork cubes served in a sweet-sour sauce and garnished with pineapple chunks, carrots, celery and green peppers.

Bo tsai gao Steamed dish of spinach, ham and bamboo shoots.

Bo tsai shiao niu ro pien Shredded veal cutlet stir-fried in ginger, scallions, soy, sherry and served on a bed of spinach.

Bo tsai ti pong Fresh boiled ham flavoured with star anise, sherry and soy served in a ring of cooked spinach.

Bocai chao zhugan Stir-fried pig's liver with spinach.

Bocai doufu tang Bean curd and spinach in chicken broth.

Bong bong gee Steamed boned chicken served with a sauce of hot peppers, ginger, sesame seed paste and vinegar.

Bor lay har kow Minced prawn balls quick-fried.

Bow yu; bao yu Abalone.

Bow yu ghuy peen tang; bao yu ji pian tang Sliced chicken, abalone and vegetables in a clear broth.

Bow yu tang; bao yu tang Abalone slices, mushrooms and celery in a clear broth.

Bu wun ju sow Pigs' feet pickled in a sweet-sour sauce.

Caihua chao roupian Marinated pork slices stir-fried with Chinese mushrooms and blanched cauliflower.

Caihua geng Thick soup of chopped cauliflower, ham, chicken meat in chicken broth with beaten eggs.

Chaah gwaah jing juh yook Pork slices steamed with tea melons.

Chaau faahn; chao fan Rice stir-fried with various combinations of vegetables and savoury meats such as Chinese roast pork, ham, bacon and Chinese sausages.

Chaau gai daan; chao ji dan Basic stir-fried eggs.

Cha gwa dun op tong Whole duck steamed with pickled cucumbers.

Cha hsia chiu Minced shrimp, pork fat, water chestnuts formed into balls, rolled in batter and deep-fried.

Cha shu Boneless butt of pork marinated in sauce of soy, sugar, hoisin sauce and slow roasted; served hot or cold or used as a garnish or stir-fried with vegetables.

Cha shu bok tsoi Chinese roast pork stir-fried with vegetables.

Cha shu chao mien Fried noodles served with a garnish of Chinese roast pork, bean sprouts, cabbage, bamboo shoots in a rich sauce.

Cha siu gai; cha shao ji Chicken is hung to dry, then cavity is filled with ingredients such as pork fat, chilli peppers, soy sauce, bean sprouts then grilled over slow flame; the crispy skin is served separately from meat and is eaten as in Peking duck wrapped in thin pancakes with scallions and cucumber strips.

Cha sung shu yu Crisp-fried fish in sweet-sour sauce.

Cha yang wei Sugar-filled pastry balls deep-fried and coated with sugar.

Cha yao hua Deep-fried kidneys and sweet peppers.

Chah daan; cha dan Hard-boiled eggs immersed in strong tea for mild smokey flavour and marble-like pattern.

Chahn peih gai; chen pi ji Boned, bite-size pieces of chicken stir-fried with soy, chilli peppers and tangerine peel.

Chan pei shiu op Roast duck flavoured with orange peel, yellow bean paste, ginger and soy sauce.

Chang jai lun ban Salad of ham, chicken, abalone, bean sprouts and cucumber dressed with soy, mustard, sesame oil.

Chao chu kan Pork liver slices stir-fried with mushrooms, onion, spinach, ginger and served in a soy-based sauce.

Chao fan Fried rice garnished with fried egg slivers and scallions.

Chao haah look Shrimps stir-fried with spring onions coated with sweet-sour sauce.

Chao hsia ren Prawns quick-fried with peas.

Chao ji gan Stir-fried chicken livers and peas.

Chao jie lan tsai Stir-fried mustard and watercress greens.

Chao muxu rou; mu hsu pork Mixture of Chinese vegetables, shredded pork and eggs, flavoured with scallions and soy, usually eaten wrapped in Mandarin pancakes.

Chao ju gan Stir-fried pork liver slices, onions and spinach flavoured with soy and wine sauce.

Chao ou pian Stir-fried sliced lotus roots, braised with mushrooms and bamboo shoots.

Chao sangai Diced chicken breast, diced pork fillet, marinated and fried separately then served with flavoured diced bamboo shoots.

Chao sarm seen; chao san hsien Stir-fried chicken slices, abalone, shrimps and vegetables.

Chao shan hu; chow seen woo Boned eel quick-fried in soy, ginger and garlic.

Chao shui ya pian Boned breast of duck fried with mushrooms and bamboo shoots.

Chao si fun Rice sticks stir-fried with Chinese mushrooms, dried shrimps and pork in chicken stock.

Chao sih ji dou Stir-fried French beans and water chestnuts.

Chao ya gan Duck liver stir-fried with bamboo shoots and mushrooms.

Chao yaohua Pork kidneys stir-fried with water chestnuts, bamboo shoots, wood ears and spinach.

Chao yu pian Fillets of bass quick-fried with ginger, onion and soy.

Chao yu sung Fried minced fish served on a bed of fried turnips.

Cheh tze niu suh Beef tongue simmered in tomato-flavoured stock, served cold.

Chen chu wan tzu Ground pork, water chestnuts, mushrooms, glutinous rice and flavourings formed into little balls and steamed.

Chen pei shiu gai Chinese roast chicken flavoured with tangerine peel, soy, yellow bean paste and ginger.

Chen pei yu yuen Tangerine-flavoured fillets of flounder shaped into balls served in broth or garnished with vegetables.

Chen pi ya Steamed duck served with savoury cooking liquid flavoured with tangerine peel, ginger, anise, soy.

Cheng chieh tzu Steamed egg-plant dressed with soy, garlic, hot pepper, oil and vinegar.

Cheng tu tzu chi Shredded marinated chicken served on a bed of blanched spinach and water chestnuts topped with cashew nuts.

Cheung Rice buns filled with lotus seeds or water chestnuts, steamed, wrapped in bamboo shoots.

Chiang jou Boned pork boiled in savoury sauce of sugar, sherry, ginger, soy, anise, cinnamon, dried tangerine peel, cloves; served sliced cold without sauce.

Chiao ma chi Boiled chicken breast served with a sprinkling of onion and ginger and a sauce of sesame seed oil, sherry, vinegar, soy and sugar.

Chieh nee Steamed mashed egg-plant stir-fried with ground pork and hot pepper.

Chiehtze hsiang Deep-fried egg-plant tossed with cooked mushrooms, bamboo shoots, chicken and ham in a soy-based sauce served garnished with peanuts or almonds.

Chiehtze shiao niu pai Veal chops simmered in tomato-flavoured sauce.

Chien hsia bing Shrimp patties served with cabbage.

Chien tsen bai tsai Steamed casserole of celery cabbage, layered with chopped flounder, chicken, ham, egg mixture.

Chiieh tsao chi ting Deep-fried rice noodles shaped into a bird's nest filled with chicken, water chestnuts, baby corn, green peppers, carrots, flavoured with soy, ginger, onions.

Chijiao chao jisi Shredded breast of chicken stir-fried with red pepper and celery flavoured with ginger, hot chilli, black bean sauce.

Chin chang peang Paper-thin layers of steamed dough for wrapping morsels of roast duck or pork crispy skin along with a piece of scallion and a spicy sauce.

Chin chien chi Chicken legs boned and stuffed with ham, steamed, then coated with batter and roasted; served sliced in coin-shaped circles.

Ching chaau ha yahn; ching chao xia ren Prawns shelled and marinated in garlic and ginger-flavoured wine and quick-fried.

Ching cheng shih yu Shad slices steamed with diced pork, smoked ham, mushrooms and bamboo shoots.

Ching chiang jou szu Shredded pork marinated in soy and sesame oil, stir-fried in sweet bean sauce and served on a bed of scallions.

Ching deuhn ap tong Duck broth garnished with ham and bamboo shoots.

Ching deuhn gai tong Clear chicken broth; chicken meat eaten separately dipped in sauce.

Ching deuhn ngauh yuhk; ching dun niu rou Slow-simmered beef sliced thin and served cold with selection of condiments, cucumber and carrot strips.

Ching do sha ding don jiao Egg omelette of shrimp, mushrooms, peas, flavoured with ginger and soy.

Ching do sha ren Stir-fried shrimp with green peas.

Ching dun chwan sao ya Duck roasted then steamed with bamboo shoots, ginger and spices, served with a thin cover of sliced Virginia ham.

Ching jao tsao niu ro Thin slices of flank steak stir-fried with green peppers in a sauce of soy, oyster sauce, sherry and ginger.

Ching jao yo yu Dried reconstituted squid stir-fried with pork and green peppers.

Ching jew chow ghuy pien; ching jiao chao ji pian Braised chicken slices, sweet peppers and scallions flavoured with red bean sauce.

Ching jiao shiao niu ro Veal steak stir-fried with green peppers.

Ching jing baak gup Squab steamed with ham, golden needles (a vegetable fungus), Chinese mushrooms, red dates, scallions and ginger.

Ching jing yuh; ching zsen yu Fresh fish rubbed with seasoning and steamed whole served on a bed of shredded vegetables.

Ching jiu gai kew Boned breast of chicken cubes marinated in soy and ginger and stir-fried with green peppers.

Ching jiu yeong ju yoke Sweet green peppers stuffed with ground pork and dried shrimp, steamed.

Ching tong gap leih; ching tang ge Clam meat steamed in ginger-flavoured chicken broth.

Ching tong yu to Clear broth of chicken flavoured with ham, bamboo shoots, mushrooms and specially treated fish tripe (dried fish stomach used as a flavouring agent).

Ching tsai ban gahn Salad of pressed bean curds and celery hearts dressed with vinegar and soy.

Ching tsao Stir-fried vegetables; **do ya** stir-fried bean sprouts; **gai lan** stir-fried broccoli; **bai tsai** stir-fried Chinese cabbage; **niu ro** stir-fried celery hearts with beef; **su tsai** stir-fried mixed Chinese vegetables.

Ching tsao sha ren Fresh shrimps stir-fried with ginger and scallions.

Ching tsen chwan gee Steamed whole chicken.

Ching tsen chwan yah Steamed whole duck.

Ching tsen dung gu Steamed Chinese mushrooms.

Ching tsen gee ro Boned breast of chicken cubes steamed with Chinese mushrooms and lily flowers.

Ching tsen yu Whole trout or bass steamed with cover of ham and mushrooms.

Ching yo bing Scallion pancakes usually served with meat dish.

Chiu niang Seasoning made of fermented rice.

Chiyou ji Chicken marinated in soy then slowly simmered in soy broth served without sauce cut into bite-size pieces.

Chizhi zheng paigu Marinated pork spare-ribs in black bean sauce garnished with red or green peppers.

Cho goo ghuy peen tang Chicken slices and mushrooms in a clear broth.

Choi faahn; cai fan Rice cooked with vegetables.

Choi yuen geong chung ghuy Chicken steamed with ginger and onion and served with braised kale.

Choi yuen hoy au ngau yuk; tsai ba hao yu hiou rou Shredded beef quick-fried with vegetables and oyster sauce.

Chop suey American version of Chinese stir-fried mixture of vegetables and roast pork.

Chow bow yu pien Abalone braised with bamboo shoots, ham, onion, Chinese mushrooms and peas flavoured with ginger, garlic and soy sauce.

Chow haah look Shrimps in shells stir-fried with scallions, ginger, garlic and hoisin sauce.

Chow to jiu pai tsai Stir-fried French beans and Chinese cabbage.

Chow yook soong Minced pork, crushed peanuts, diced water chestnuts, Chinese mushrooms and sugar peas flavoured with ginger and soy sauce.

Chow yu; chao yu Whole fish simmered in pan with ginger, scallions and wine.

Chu hua chi shun Chicken gizzards marinated in rice wine and deep-fried with garlic, chilis and sesame seed oil.

Chuan cheh gwa Deep-fried whole bass in sauce of chopped pork and shrimp-flavoured savoury sauce.

Chue tu Pig's stomach stuffed with barley and steamed.

Chuen gnau peen tang; juan niou pian tang Beef slices and vegetables in clear broth.

Chuen jien Pork-filled egg rolls cooked over smoking grill.

Chuen kuen Egg skins filled with bamboo shoots, shrimp, pork, water chestnuts, spring onions and deep-fried.

Chui pi gai Chicken legs simmered in marinade of soy and ginger, and deep-fried.

Chui pi yu Crispy fried bass in sweet-sour sauce.

Chung bao yang ro Lamb stir-fried with scallions and flavoured with soy, garlic, anise-pepper and sesame seed oil.

Chung hwa don tsao fan Scallion and egg fried rice.

Chung maih gun pin; cong mi gun pihn Quick-fried pork liver served smothered in braised onions.

Chung sar tan pao Flavoured mushrooms, ham and rice folded into egg pancakes.

Chung sik ngau lau Sliced beef steak, quick-fried and flavoured with soy and tomato sauce.

Chung siu ap; cong shao yu Whole duck stuffed with onion and slow-simmered in broth.

Chunng baau yeuhng yuhk; cong bao yang rou pian Marinated lamb slices quick-fried and served on a bed of spring onions.

Chuy mow faah Stir-fried ribbons of sweet pastry.

Congee Rice gruel usually mildly flavoured with additions of meat, fish or other seafood and eaten as a snack or for breakfast; **tien shi fan** sweet congee of lotus seeds, raisins, dates and sugar; **shi fan** traditional congee lightly flavoured with mushrooms and soy; **gai jook** chicken congee; **ju yoke jook** pork congee; **yu san jook** fish congee.

Congyou ya Slow-simmered whole duck with Chinese mushrooms, bamboo shoots flavoured with chopped scallions.

Da shieh fu yung don Egg omelette with King crab meat.

Da to tsai tsao ro si Shredded pork stir-fried with kohlrabi flavoured with dried shrimps.

Da tow tsai tsao niu ro si Shredded beef stir-fried with kohlrabi.

Dan hwa tong Egg drop soup.

Dauh gu chaau yauh yuh; dou gu chao yu yu Pieces of squid stir-fried in sauce of ginger, garlic, soy and black beans.

Dauh gu gai; dou gu ji Bite-size pieces of chicken stir-fried with black bean sauce, garlic, tangerine peel, soy.

Dauh ngah chaau yuhk si; dou ya chao rou si Bean sprouts stir-fried with shredded pork flavoured with pepper, soy.

Deih si maht; yang rou pian Thinly sliced leg of lamb quick-fried with ginger, soy, rice wine.

Dim sum Snack foods usually of filled steamed or fried buns, stuffed egg skins or grilled meats to be taken as finger foods at brunch or tea; **cha chu kuen** fried spring roll; **cha shiu pao** buns stuffed with pork; **dung gu ro bao** pork mushroom bun; **fen kuo** crab dumpling; **fun gwor** shrimp and vegetable bun; **fun goh** mushroom, roast pork and cabbage filled buns; **fa sun jiong cha shu bao** roast pork filled buns flavoured with peanut butter; **fahn shu dan** sweet potato balls; **go te** fried Chinese ravioli; **gow li dow sa** deep-fried flour puffs filled with sweet bean paste; **gee bao** steamed buns filled with chicken, oyster sauce mixture; **ga li gai guen** curried chicken rolls; **ga li goh** curried beef triangles; **ha won ton** shrimp won ton; **hung lo bo ro bao** pork and carrot filled steamed buns; **hwa jwen** steamed sweet buns; **har gew** shrimp dumplings; **ha yoke fo twei to si** shrimp toast with ham; **hai shu mai** crab-, pork-, vegetable-filled steamed dumplings; **ho yu cha shu bao** pork-stuffed steamed bun with oyster sauce; **hwa sun jiang tong yuen** New Year cake of mushrooms, shrimp, ham, water chestnuts filling in glutinous rice pastry shaped into half moons; **ham sui kok** fried dumpling; **har kau** shrimp dumpling; **hsia jen tu sau** deep-fried prawn toast; **jao tze** Chinese ravioli filled with beef or pork and cabbage; **jien ngo bang** lotus root cakes; **jiao yen sha** rice flour coated shrimp deep-fried; **kai yang niu pa** dried shrimpburgers; **lien ngo yoke bang** fried lotus root cakes; **lo bok gow** steamed turnip cake; **ma tai har gow** steamed dumplings filled with shrimp and water chestnuts; **niu ro tong bao** beef-filled steamed buns; **ngo bing** lotus root chips; **ngo yoke fun goh** steamed buns filled with beef and water chestnuts; **nam yu cha shu bao** steamed buns filled with roast pork and red bean curd cheese; **pai kwat** steamed spare ribs; **shang ling** crisp-fried bean curd skins filled with pork; **sha twe mein bao** deep-fried shrimp toast; **si shi sha bing** deep-fried shrimp cakes; **shu mai** steamed pork-stuffed pastry; **sun ee bing** fried potato, tomato and egg patties; **tza won ton** fried won tons; **tza sue won ton** won ton skins fried in sugar; **tsu ro tong bao** pork-filled steamed buns; **tza bai nahn gwa** fried butternut squash; **tsing ngau yuk** steamed beef ball in lotus leaf; **won ton** pork- and water chestnut-filled skins; **yo tiao** deep-fried pastry puffs.

Ding how tsao don Chinese scrambled eggs with shredded meat and lettuce heart.

Don bi yu guan bo tsai Egg skins filled with minced fish served on a bed of spinach.

Donggu dun ji Whole chicken simmered in broth with mushrooms served in broth.

Donggu zheng zigi Bite-size pieces of boned chicken steamed with Chinese dried mushrooms.

Dongsun chao rousi Boned pork stir-fried with bamboo shoots.

Doong gwaah joong Whole steamed winter melon filled with chicken meat and broth.

Douya chao rousi Bean sprouts stir-fried with shredded pork.

Dow ban jiong yu Whole carp or sea bass steamed in sauce flavoured with brown bean paste.

Dow chow juh yook Lima beans braised with pork.

Dow fu fan keh Bean curd with tomato.

Dow fu gahn ban ro tsai Pressed bean curd and spinach salad.

Dow fu gahn ching tsai ro si Pressed bean curd and celery with stir-fried beef.

Dow fu gai tsai tong Soup of bean curd and mustard greens in chicken broth.

Dow fu gee tong Bean curds in chicken soup.

Dow fu gee tza Bean curd with chicken giblets braised in soy-ginger sauce.

Dow fu go tsai Spinach stir-fried with fermented bean cake.

Dow fu mun ju yoke Bean curds braised with minced pork and black mushrooms.

Dow fu mun li yu Whole carp served with rich pork-flavoured sauce and soy bean cakes.

Dow fu niu ro Bean curd with beef slices.

Dow fu swan la tong Rich, heavy soup with bean curds, water chestnuts, bamboo shoots, mushrooms in hot and spicy pork broth.

Dow fu tsao sha ren Stir-fried shrimp with bean curd.

Dow fu tsen niu ro Bean curd steamed with minced beef.

Dow fu tsen tsu ro Bean curd steamed with minced pork.

Dow gock chow juh yook String beans braised with pork.

Dow see loong haah Lobster chopped with shell simmered in pork and black bean sauce.

Dow si pai gwut Spare-ribs steamed in black bean sauce.

Dow si shiu pai gwut Spare-ribs braised in black bean sauce.

Dow si tsing ju yoke Steamed minced pork with salted black beans.

Dun baak gup Squabs simmered with winter melon and mushrooms.

Dun gee; tze fung gee Steamed chicken with mushrooms in broth.

Dun op tong Steamed duck soup garnished with bamboo shoots, mushrooms, ham and ginger.

Dung gee Whole chicken steamed and allowed to jell in broth.

Dung gu dow fu Bean curd braised with black mushrooms.

Dung gu gee chiu Boned breast of chicken stir-fried with ginger and Chinese mushrooms.

Dung gu go ba tong Soup of Chinese mushrooms in chicken broth.

Dung gu hai sun Stir-fried sea cucumber and mushrooms in chicken broth sauce garnished with shredded turkey breast.

Dung gu heh tze Chinese mushroom caps stuffed with ground pork mixture served on a bed of spinach or cabbage.

Dung gu hwa tsai Braised cauliflower with mushrooms.

Dung gu mun gee Chicken and mushroom casserole.

Dung gu sha ren Stir-fried shrimp with mushrooms.

Dung gu tsao don Mushroom omelette.

Dung gwa tsung Soup of winter melon in rich chicken broth garnished with bamboo shoots, mushrooms, ham, shrimp, chicken.

Dung po yeuhng yuhk; dong po yang rou Marinated lamb chunks stewed in marinade with potatoes and carrots added to cook in the savoury broth; served in bowls.

Dung seun siu jyu; dong sun shao rou Red-cooked belly of pork (pork simmered in soy-flavoured broth) served with bamboo shoot slices.

Dung sun gee tong Chicken soup with bamboo shoots.

Dung sun gee yung sha Marinated shrimps stir-fried, then combined with minced chicken, egg whites and mushrooms.

Dung sun pai gu Spare-ribs simmered with bamboo shoots.

Dung tee Jellied pigs' knuckles flavoured with ginger.

Dung tsoi yah Slow-simmered duck flavoured with preserved celery cabbage served with mushrooms.

Dzao tze mun yang chung Slow-simmered beef shank with stir-fried onions.

Faahn gwaah ngow yook Braised squash flavoured with beef and black bean sauce.

Faahn keh chow ngow yook Stir-fried beef and tomatoes in sauce garnished with fried potatoes and onions.

Faat tsoi pa op Duck deep-fried with seaweed.

Fan cheh ro pien Pork slices stir-fried with tomato slices.

Fan keh shu tzai gai Stir-fried chicken pieces with tomatoes and potatoes.

Fangie roupian tang Pork and tomato soup.

Fei chwee yoke ding Diced pork tenderloin stir-fried with bamboo shoots and snow peas.

Fong wo dow fu Bean cakes stir-fried with mushrooms, bamboo shoots, flavoured with dried shrimps and preserved tea melon.

Foo yoong daahn Rich scrambled eggs with various shredded meats and vegetables.

Foong lut ghuy Chicken pieces and chestnuts simmered in rich broth.

Fu gwa dow si har Shrimp stir-fried with bitter melon and salted black beans.

Fu gwa gno yoke do si jiong Beef slices stir-fried with bitter melon in black bean sauce.

Fu gwa mun pai gwut Spare-ribs simmered in black bean sauce with bitter melon.

Fu gwa si yu Whole shad steamed in black bean sauce to which is added bitter melon.

Fu gwa yoke si Pork slices stir-fried with bitter melon and flavoured with black bean sauce.

Fu pi hung sao yu Whole carp covered with bean curd skins steamed in ginger-flavoured sauce.

Fu yong dai hai King crab meat egg fu yong.

Fu yong gai Chicken omelette.

Fu yong hai yoke dung gu Crab omelette.

Fu yu don Scrambled eggs with fermented bean cake.

Fu yu sang tsoi Lettuce stir-fried with fermented bean cake.

Fu yu tsing ju yoke Pork loin slices steamed with fermented bean cake flavouring.

Fu yu yah Duck simmered in savoury stock flavoured with fermented bean cake.

Fu yung gai pien Fried batter-coated strips of chicken breasts served with stir-fried peas and mushrooms.

Fu yung gee pien Chicken breasts stir-fried with ginger, mushrooms and Chinese cabbage.

Fun see juh yook daahn Scrambled eggs with cellophane noodles garnished with pork and ham.

Fun tsen dung gu gee Chicken breasts covered with rice flour and steamed mushrooms.

Fun tsen nan gwa niu ro Beef slices marinated in soy and brown bean sauce steamed with pumpkin.

Fun tsen niu ro Beef tenderloin slices marinated in soy-brown bean sauce and steamed.

Fun tsen pai gu Spare-ribs coated with rice flour and steamed.

Fun tsen tien sao niu ro Beef slices steamed with sweet potatoes.

Fun tsen tsu pai Pork chops coated with rice flour and steamed.

Fun tsen wu shiang gee Chicken pieces coated with rice flour and steamed.

Fung wei sha Jumbo shrimp covered in batter and deep-fried.

Furong ji Minced chicken meat coated in egg-white batter and deep-fried.

Ga li gai Chicken curry.

Ga li tong mien Curry soup with noodles.

Gaai laan chow dhaah sieu Chinese broccoli braised with Chinese roast pork in light sauce.

Gahn bei sao lo bo si Dried scallops stir-fried with shredded turnips.

Gahn jien sha Shelled shrimps stir-fried with hoisin sauce.

Gahn jien yu Lightly battered fish fried with ginger, scallions and spices.

Gahn tsao sha Shelled shrimps stir-fried until glazed with ginger-soy sauce.

Gai fan Rice cooked with chicken and mushrooms.

Gai kow sub gum Boned chicken breast pieces stir-fried with bamboo shoots, water chestnuts, celery and peas, served in chicken broth sauce and topped with almonds.

Gai lan ju yoke jeong Broccoli stir-fried with mushrooms.

Gai lan ju yoke heong Mustard greens with minced pork sauce.

Gai lan shiao niu ro Stir-fried veal cutlet with broccoli.

Gai lan yu pien Flounder fillets stir-fried with Chinese broccoli in oyster sauce.

Gai si dow fu Shredded bean curd stir-fried with bamboo shoots, mushrooms, water chestnuts, cooked shredded chicken and ham.

Gai si sang tsoi Minced chicken, mushrooms, bamboo shoots and celery stir-fried and served on a bed of lettuce.

Gai si yu chi Shark fins boiled in chicken broth with shredded chicken meat and flavourings.

Gai tsai dow fu tong Soup of mustard greens and bean curds.

Gai tsoi ju yoke tong Pork soup with mustard greens.

Gai yung Mixture of minced chicken and egg quick-fried, served with chicken stock gravy.

Gai yung sok mai tong Chicken and corn soup.

Gan li yah Stewed duck with chestnuts.

Gan shao niou rou tsu Shredded beef quick-fried with green peppers and transparent noodles in light sauce.

Ganjian jipu Boned chicken breast, marinated, coated in batter and fried, served with tomato-sesame oil sauce.

Gee jiu lu sun Boned chicken pieces fried in hot spicy sauce served with asparagus.

Gee pien dung gu tong Soup of chicken, mushroom and bamboo shoots.

Gee ro bai tsai tong Chicken soup with celery cabbage.

Gee si tsao fan Cooked rice stir-fried with turkey or chicken meat, onion and peas.

Gee tong mien Chicken noodle soup.

Gee yo tsai shing Stir-fried cabbage flavoured with chicken fat.

Gee yung sha Marinated shrimps, minced chicken and eggs scrambled and served with ham and asparagus.

Geong chung dow see ghuy Quick-fried chopped chicken with ginger and black bean sauce.

Geong chung ngau yuk Quick-fried beef slices with ginger and onion.

Geung chung wo daaih; cong jiang guo da xia Cracked whole crab cooked in sauce of ginger, onion and minced pork.

Geung chung wo luhng ha; jiang cong guo lon xia Cracked whole lobster cooked in sauce of ginger, onion and minced pork.

Gez sung Coarsely minced pigeon fried with water chestnuts, served on a bed of thin fried noodles.

Ghuy daahn gow Egg pouches filled with minced pork and covered with ginger-oyster sauce.

Ghuy gwat jeung Small pieces of chicken stewed with soy and sugar.

Ghuy yoong low sun Chicken broth thickened with minced chicken meat and asparagus pulp.

Ghuy yoong yien waw Bird's nest soup—chicken broth thickened with gelatinous threads of bird's nest and minced chicken meat.

Ghuy yow lay ju Carp or sea bass fried in chicken fat, chilli sauce, ginger and simmered in chicken broth served with bean curds.

Giang yo Ginger oil.

Ging gee niu ro tong Beef broth.

Go sao ya tze Steamed duck, boned and deep-fried.

Go sao yu Whole fish stuffed with pork and ginger, fried.

Go tsup ngo yoke Beef cubes flavoured with ginger and brown bean sauce stewed in orange and lemon juice.

Gon chaau ha dyuhn Whole prawns stir-fried until shells are crusted with the ginger-soy sauce in which they are fried.

Gone siu dung sun Fried bamboo shoots flavoured with salted vegetables.

Gone siu yee dung Quick-fried mushrooms and bamboo shoots.

Gone siu yee sung Shredded dried scallops deep-fried with broccoli leaves.

Gong yu chee ju gyok tong Soup of pigs' knuckles flavoured with dried scallops.

Goo lo yuk Batter-covered bite-size pieces of pork deep-fried and covered with a sweet-sour sauce.

Gow chung go Rice flour and sugar pudding steamed in nine layers.

Gow far ghuy Chicken stuffed with minced pork and vegetables wrapped in lotus leaves and baked in clay.

Guk fa wo; ju hua guo A communal hot-pot in which are boiled a selection of meats and vegetables from which diners help themselves.

Gum chien Fried minced pork and crab meat patties.

Guo shao ji Boned chicken breast coated in light egg batter and deep-fried.

Guo shao niou rou Beef boiled in broth of onion, ginger and soy, coated in batter and deep-fried.

Guy gon tong Soup of chicken innards and Chinese cabbage.

Guy yung don tat Steamed dish of egg and minced chicken.

Gwaah hee choy tong Soup of Chinese watercress and minced pork.

Gwai gei ghuy Chicken pieces quick-fried then simmered with bamboo shoot slices in soy and sugar sauce.

Ha mai bok tsoi tong Cabbage soup with dried shrimp in pork or chicken stock.

Haahm daan; xian dan Duck eggs immersed in brine for 30-40 days, boiled, eaten plain or used as a garnish or to add flavour to egg, pork or vegetable dishes.

Haahm joong Savoury filling of glutinous rice, lotus seeds, green peas, mushrooms, roast pork, bacon wrapped in dried corn leaves (lotus leaves when available) and simmered; a festive dish.

Haahm shia Shrimp.

Haaih wohng yuh chi; xie huang yu chi Shark's fin simmered in rich stock with addition of crab meat, crab eggs, rice wine and lard.

Haap to ghuy Marinated chicken fillets quick-fried with walnuts and ham.

Hahng yahn dauh fuh sai gwa jung; xing ren dou fu xi gua zhong Creamy drink of ground rice, ground almonds, water and sugar.

Hahng yahn dauh fuh sai gwa jung; xing ren dou fu xi gua zhong Almond jelly with nuts in a water-melon shell.

Hai sun sao Sea cucumber and black mushrooms in chicken soup with Chinese cabbage garnish.

Hai yoke dow fu Bean curd simmered in chicken broth with peas, crab meat and mushrooms.

Hai yoke fu yong don Elaborate omelette of crab meat, bamboo shoots, mushrooms and water chestnuts.

Hai yoke tsao don Eggs stir-fried with crab meat and water chestnuts.

Hai yung shok mai gung Crab meat and corn in chicken broth.

Ham don tseng ju yoke Minced pork steamed with salt egg.

Ham don yoke bang tsing lung ha Steamed lobster with rich sauce based on minced pork, ginger, soy and water chestnuts.

Ham tan Eggs cured in mixture of lye, straw pieces and salt, placed in a crock for a few months; served uncooked, sliced thin with pickled ginger; pungent, cheesy flavour.

Ham tsoi dow fu Stir-fried bean curds simmered in broth with chopped preserved mustard greens.

Ham yu tsen yoke bang Minced pork steamed with salt fish.

Han yen dow fu bo lo Almond jelly with pineapple, cherries and litchis.

Hang yang peang Almond cake, baked as a thick cookie.

Hang yang wu Sweet, almond-flavoured soup served as a dessert with cake.

Hao yu chieh lan tsai Stir-fried broccoli in oyster sauce.

Hao yiu niu jou Marinated beef slices first deep-fried then stir-fried with ginger, scallion and oyster sauce.

Hao yu ge sung Minced pigeon quick-fried with oyster sauce, mushrooms and peas, eaten rolled in lettuce leaf.

Hao yu pa peng Chicken wings braised in oyster sauce with ginger served with stir-fried broccoli.

Har gow Chopped shrimp, water chestnuts, bamboo shoots formed into balls deep-fried and served with oyster-based sauce.

Har yee kai Whole chicken stuffed with mushrooms, pickled cabbage, herbs, onions and wrapped in lotus leaves, encased in clay and baked.

Har yen dow fu Stir-fried shrimp and bean curd flavoured with soy, ginger and brown bean sauce.

Har yoke yuan ju bok tsoi Shrimp and pork meatballs simmered in chicken broth with mushrooms, cabbage, ginger and scallions.

Har yuan tong Shrimp meatballs in pork broth with cabbage, mushrooms and water chestnuts.

Hatzee lung ha joing Shrimp with lobster sauce (sauce of minced pork, salted black beans and soy in soup stock thickened with eggs).

Haw lo yu; he yu River bass.

Haw yeep faahn Filling of rice, roast pork, Chinese sausages, dried pork, dried duck, dried scallops, peanuts, water chestnuts, bamboo shoots and mushrooms flavoured with soy and scallions wrapped in corn leaves (lotus leaves when available) and steamed.

Heh tao gee ding Boned breast of chicken coated with batter and fried served with fried walnuts.

Heh tao shiao niu ro ding Marinated veal cutlet served with deep-fried walnut halves.

Heh tao yao hwa Pork kidneys and walnuts deep-fried separately and served with Szechuan ground pepper.

Heong chong tsing gai Chicken steamed with Chinese mushrooms and Chinese sausages in soy- and sherry-based sauce.

Heong jiao bang Banana pancakes.

Heong tsong noh mai Glutinous rice with diced Chinese sausage and dried black mushrooms flavoured with soy.

Heung wat san yu kow Minced fish balls quick-fried with mixed vegetables.

Hey bai dow sha Sweet bean paste topped with whipped cream and maraschino cherries.

High par sin goo Crab meat and stewed mushrooms with an egg-white sauce.

Ho go Fire pot of boiling meat stock in which are dipped bite-size pieces of chicken, beef, pork, shrimp and vegetables such as spinach, lettuce, cabbage, watercress by the diner, served with sauce of his choice such as soy, oyster, duck, hoisin, etc.

Hoi how sieu Deep-fried New Year cake.

Hoi shien jiong gai Boiled chicken served with hoisin sauce.

Hoisin jiong siu pai gwut Spare-ribs baked in hoisin sauce.

Hoisin tou yen gai Chicken breast cubes stir-fried with blanched almonds in hoisin and soy-based sauce.

Holan dow tsao gai yoke Boned chicken pieces stir-fried with snow peas, mushrooms and water chestnuts.

Hom har tsing ju yoke Pork slices steamed with ginger and shrimp paste flavouring.

Hong yen dan ta Fried almond custard.

Hongmen jichi Chicken wings simmered in soy-sherry based sauce with ginger and scallions served in a ring of bamboo shoots and mushrooms braised in the chicken liquid.

Hongshao rouwan Pork and water chestnut meatballs fried then simmered in chicken broth with Chinese cabbage and cellophane noodles.

Hoongsieu juy yook; hao yiou niou rou Casserole of diced pork, with leeks and onions served on a bed of braised spinach.

Hoongyu; hung yu Red snapper.

Hotwei ban yang tsai Salad of shredded ham, chicken, cucumber, agar agar strips and bean sprouts dressed with soy and sesame oil.

Hotwei don chuen Minced ham, pork and ginger in egg skins fried and simmered in stock, served on celery cabbage leaves.

Hotwei tsao fan Fried rice with ham, eggs and peas.

Hotwei tsen dung gwa Ham steamed with winter melon, ginger and scallions.

Houh yauh ngauh yuhk; hao you niu rou Marinated beef slices quick-fried in oyster sauce served in its own rich sauce.

How yo dow fu Bean curd stir-fried with sauce of soy, stock and oyster sauce.

How yo yang twei Leg of lamb marinated with oyster sauce and roasted.

How yo tien gee Frogs' legs simmered in meat stock flavoured with ginger and oyster sauce.

How yo yo yu Squid simmered in ginger and oyster sauce.

How yu shiao niu pai Veal chops simmered with ginger, scallion and soy-oyster sauce.

How yu shiao niu ro Stir-fried veal steak with oyster sauce and Chinese mushrooms, snow peas and bamboo shoots.

Hoyau ngau yuk; hao yiou niou rou Thinly sliced beef, marinated in wine, oil, cornflour and baking soda, quick-fried in oyster sauce.

Hoylo yu; hai yu Sea bass.

Hoyow bao yu Abalone in oyster sauce.

Hoyow tow yu pien Abalone braised in oyster-soy sauce garnished with ham.

Hoyow do fu Bean curds simmered with scallions and oyster sauce.

Hoyow gai yik Chicken wings simmered in oyster sauce broth.

Hoyow har kew Chopped shrimp, water chestnuts, bamboo shoots formed into balls, deep-fried and served with an oyster-based sauce.

Hoyow ngo yoke Bite-size pieces of flank steak stir-fried in oyster-based sauce.

Hoyow shiu ngo pa Steak smeared with oyster sauce and grilled.

Hoyow yu yuen Fish balls braised with mushrooms, bamboo shoots and peas in oyster sauce.

Hoysin cheung Seafood sauce.

Hoysum; hai yu Sea slugs.

Hoyu fung gon Chicken livers stir-fried with bamboo shoots, Chinese mushrooms, snow peas, ginger, garlic and oyster sauce.

Hsiang ching chiao Green peppers stuffed with shrimp and beef, simmered in broth flavoured with black bean sauce.

Hsiang gu chun ji Whole chicken steamed with mushrooms, ginger and scallions.

Hsiang su ya Crispy and aromatic duck first rubbed with seasoning, pressed with onion- and ginger-flavoured soy sauce, steamed then deep-fried, served with roasted peppers and steamed rolls.

Hsiaren chao mi fen Rice stick noodles quick-fried with celery and prawns.

Hsien chou Chicken, water chestnuts, sweet potatoes and carrots in flavoured rice gruel.

Hsieh rou ban huang gua Crab meat and cucumber salad with sesame oil, soy and vinegar dressing.

Hsieh rou dow fu Quick-fried bean curd simmered with crab meat in chicken stock.

Hsieh rou yu jr tang Shark's fin soup with crab meat.

Hsien gan bei yao hua Quick-fried scallops and pork kidneys.

Hsien tsai tsan dou Fried broad beans and mustard and cress greens braised in chicken stock.

Hsing ren dou fu Curd of sweet and bitter almonds and rice covered with syrup and decorated with sliced cherries.

Hsun dan Boiled eggs marinated in soy, sesame oil, sugar and hickory-smoked salt.

Hsun yu Marinated fish deep-fried and braised in stock with soy and sugar until fish appears 'smoked'.

Hua jiao rou wan-z Pork balls seasoned with spices and wine, deep-fried.

Huang gua juan ji tang Chicken and cucumber soup.

Huang gwa ro pien tong Pork chop soup with cucumbers.

Huang yu geng; wong yu gong Thick soup of yellow fish and bean curd.

Huasum tzu chi Diced chicken leg quick-fried with peanuts, chillis, ginger, garlic, soy and vinegar.

Hueng so ghuy toi; hsiang su ji tuei Marinated chicken legs, deep-fried.

Hueng so chuen ngaap; hsiang tsu chuan ji Marinated chicken deep-fried three times for a crispy skin.

Hui wan dou Peas braised with mushrooms, bamboo shoots and garnished with ham.

Hung lo bo hung sao niu ro Shank of beef slow-cooked in soy-based stock with addition of carrots in last half hour of cooking.

Hung par teen ngaap Duck fried then simmered with soy and sugar.

Hung sao bao pien Braised sliced abalone in sauce of chicken broth, soy and sherry.

Hung sao bing tang ti pong Fresh ham slow-cooked in soy-based broth.

Hung sao dow fu yu Whole fish slow-cooked with bean curds in soy-based sauce.

Hung sao gee Chicken braised in meat stock and soy with bamboo shoots, mushrooms, ginger and scallions.

Hung sao hai sun Sea cucumbers (seafood vegetable) cooked with ham, chicken or pork in soy and oyster sauce.

Hung sao li-tze gee Chicken stewed with chestnuts in ginger-soy flavoured broth.

Hung sao niu ro Beef shank slow-cooked in soy-based broth.

Hung sao niu seh to Beef tongue slow-cooked in soy-based liquid.

Hung sao niu wei Oxtail slow-cooked in soy-based broth with tomatoes.

Hung sao pai gu Braised spare-ribs in ginger-soy sauce.

Hung sao ro Pork simmered in soy-based broth served with celery cabbage steamed in the same broth.

Hung sao tsu suh Pork tongue slow-cooked in soy-based broth.

Hung sao wu siang ro Fresh ham slow-cooked in flavoured spicy broth of anise, ginger and soy.

Hung sao yang ro Leg of lamb stew flavoured with soy and ginger, served with cooked carrots.

Hung sao yang yu Potatoes fried then simmered in soy broth.

Hung sao yu Whole sea bass slow-cooked in soy-based sauce with vegetables such as mushrooms, bamboo shoots, ginger and scallions.

Hung shao duie hsia Prawns, ginger and onions simmered in soy and wine sauce.

Hung shao du-z Tripe cooked in seasoned broth then quick-fried with greens in wine, soy and sugar sauce.

Hung shao guei yu Fried mandarin fish, braised with mushrooms, fat pork and bamboo shoots in a meat stock.

Hung shao li tzu bai tsai Stir-fried hearts of Chinese cabbage, mushrooms and chestnuts.

Hung shao niou rou Stewed shin of beef simmered with soy and wine.

Hung shao pa pao chi Chicken stuffed with Chinese sausage, mushrooms, glutinous rice and flavourings, deep-fried, cut into bite-size pieces and served with sauce of soy, ginger, scallions and star anise.

Hung shao pa ya Duck slow-cooked in broth of soy, ginger, sesame oil, onion and mushrooms.

Hung shao ti bang Braised shoulder of pork, simmered with soy, anise and wine served with braised mushrooms.

Hung shao tutze Pork tripe boiled in vinegar then deep-fried and simmered with spring onions and greens in soy, sugar and sherry.

Hung shao tui hsia Prawns in shell simmered with ginger, scallions and soy-sherry sauce until shells are coated with sauce.

Hung siu baau yuh; hong shao bao yu Abalone quick-braised in red-cooked (soy-based broth) pork liquid.

Hung siu bark kwan Mushrooms braised in soy sauce.

Hung siu bau chee Shark's fin stewed in meat sauce.

Hung siu dow fu hoi sen Sea cucumber and bean curds in heavy sauce of chicken stock thickened with eggs.

Hung siu gai; hong shao ji Red-cooked chicken (simmered in soy and water).

Hung siu hoi sum Braised sea cucumber (seafood vegetable) cooked with sliced pork, mushrooms, bamboo shoots, shrimps and seasonings in rich chicken broth.

Hung siu ju giok Pigs' feet slow-cooked in soy-based stock.

Hung siu jyu touh; hong shao zhu du Pork tripe slowly cooked in rich sauce of soy, sugar, ginger, garlic and spices, eaten for its firm but squashy texture as well as for its flavour.

Hung siu jyu yuhk; hong shao zhu rou Belly pork slowly simmered in soy-based broth rendering a rich, gelatinous gravy.

Hung siu ngauh touh; hong shao ngiu du Boiled beef tripe simmered with onion, ginger, soy, lard and rice wine.

Hung siu ngauh yuhk; hong shao niu rou Beef cubes slow-cooked in soy-based broth served with turnips or carrots cooked in the same broth.

Hung siu paaih gwat; hong shao pai ku Pork spare-ribs simmered in rich sauce of onion, garlic, ginger, soy and sherry.

Hung siu tuhk, hong shao yu Seasoned, shallow-fried fish gently simmered in sauce of soy, sugar, sherry and onions.

Hung siu yeuhng yuhk; hong shao yang rou Lamb simmered in soy-based sauce, cut into bite-size pieces and served in its own rich gravy.

Hung siu yuh chi; hong shao yu chi Soaked and simmered shark's fin re-cooked in rich meat stock or red-cooked meat gravy served garnished with shredded ham.

Hung sow li tze bai tsai Braised chestnuts, celery cabbage and Chinese mushrooms.

Hung tseng go - Apricot pudding.

Hung tsup don Fried eggs with Chinese brown sauce.

Hup toe yuk deng; he tao rou ding Quick-fried diced pork with walnuts.

Hwang gwa bong bong gee Sweet and sour boned breast of chicken served over sweet and sour cucumbers.

Hwang gwa gee tza tong Soup of chicken giblets and cucumber in chicken broth.

Hwang gwa ro pien Pork slices stir-fried with soy, ginger and sliced cucumbers.

Hwang sun gee ding Diced, boned chicken breasts stir-fried with peanuts and spices.

Hwatsai tsen gee Bite-size pieces of chicken meat steamed with cauliflower.

Hwasun jiang yaw pien Pork kidneys boiled in ginger-flavoured broth and served with peanut butter-flavoured sauce on a bed of lettuce hearts.

Hwei gwo ro Double-cooked pork slices stir-fried with sweet peppers and hot chillis flavoured with brown bean sauce.

Ja ba kwai; ja bart fie Chicken marinated and deep-fried, served with a mixture of roasted crushed Chinese red pepper and flavoured salt.

Ja hsia chiu Fried shrimp balls.

Ja la-z ji ding; chow lart ji ghuy Quick-fried diced chicken and green peppers served with soy and chilli sauce.

Ja li niu ro Beef curry.

Jaah baak gup; chao bai ge Deep-fried marinated pigeon or squab.

Jaak taai Pigs' feet boned and stuffed with sliced pork, simmered with garlic, ginger and anise served on a bed of braised spinach.

Jar chun gone; ja jen gan Deep-fried chicken gizzards and duck livers with vegetables.

Jarp kum sar wor Mixed meats and vegetables in broth served as an entrée.

Jee bow ghuy; jr bao ji Slices of chicken and ham dipped in sugar, soy, cornstarch, oil and wine, wrapped in paper and deep-fried.

Jee tsoi tong Seaweed soup thickened with egg.

Jeng tai tsai duan Steamed beaten eggs flavoured with scallions, mushrooms or minced meat.

Jeng tai tsai duan Steamed Tientsin cabbage soup garnished with ham.

Jeung ngau yuk yau bau har; jiang niou rou yiou Slices of beef stewed in soy, sugar and aniseed served mixed with quick-fried shrimps.

Ji dan chao hsi hung shr Tomato omelette.

Jia ting Peking ya Peking roast duck—a dish for special occasions; duck is specially treated, hung and coated with molasses and hoisin sauce, baked to produce a crispy skin which is peeled off and served separately with thin pancakes, hoisin sauce and scallions. The meat is served as a separate entrée with its own accompanying sauce.

Jian bao ji ding Stir-fried chicken cubes in a hoisin and yellow bean sauce.

Jian doubian yu Fish steaks marinated in soy, yellow bean sauce, sherry and fried.

Jian yo gee Whole chicken cooked in soy broth in such a manner that chicken is just cooked, served in bite-size pieces.

Jian yo sao yang pai Lamb marinated in soy, sherry and barbecued.

Jiang bao gee Boned boiled chicken stir-fried with bamboo shoots and black mushrooms simmered in stock, soy and sherry sauce.

Jiang bao niu ro mein Beef slices in flavourful sauce of brown bean, soy, hoisin and dried black mushrooms mixed with noodles.

Jiang bao ro ding Chicken breast coated with light batter, stir-fried with bamboo shoots and hot peppers and simmered in soy, sugar, brown bean sauce.

Jiang bao rou ding Stir-fried pork cubes in soy bean jam sauce.

Jiang bao shiao niu ro Diced veal cutlets stir-fried with asparagus in a brown bean, sugar, sherry and soy sauce.

Jiang bao yang ro pien Lamb slices stir-fried with ginger, garlic and scallion served in brown bean sauce.

Jiang gee Whole chicken, rubbed with marinade of brown bean sauce and soy, and simmered with ginger and scallion in marinade.

Jiang sih niu ro Flank steak slices stir-fried with treated ginger covered with sauce of slightly thickened broth, soy and sherry.

Jiang tze chieh tze Egg-plant simmered in ginger juice and shrimp-flavoured soy sauce.

Jiang tze niu ro Ginger beef tea.

Jiang tze niu ro huang dow ya Ginger beef tea with cabbage or sprouts.

Jiang yah Duck simmered in soy broth flavoured with cinnamon, star anise, rock sugar and sesame oil.

Jiang yo dow fu Bean curd with soy sauce and scallions.

Jiang yo gee Chicken legs and wings simmered in soy-wine broth.

Jiang yo sao gee Marinated chicken barbecued.

Jiang yo sao ro Marinated pork chops barbecued.

Jiang yo sao yah Marinated duck barbecued.

Jiang yo sao yang pai Marinated lamb chops barbecued.

Jiang yo yah Duck simmered in soy broth.

Jiao cheh niu ro Stir-fried flank steak strips with green peppers and tomatoes in soy-sherry sauce.

Jiao chieh shiao niu ro pien Veal cutlets stir-fried with tomatoes and green peppers in a sauce of soy, sugar, sesame oil.

Jiao ma ji Boiled breast of chicken, sliced and served with sesame oil and wine sauce.

Jiao yen ro pien Pork tenderloin coated in light batter, deep-fried and served with anise pepper salt.

Jichi hui jielan Chicken wings marinated in soy, lemon juice, sherry, ginger, fried and served with stir-fried broccoli.

Jiecai chao jiding Diced chicken pieces coated in light batter, stir-fried with ginger, spring onions, mushrooms and green peppers, flavoured with soy and sherry.

Jieh maah bang; jr ma bing Sesame seed biscuits.

Jielan chao xiaqiu Shrimp in shells, marinated in soy, ginger, sherry, cornstarch and egg whites, stir-fried with scallions and broccoli pieces.

Jien bien yu pien Flounder fillets coated with egg batter and fried.

Jien cheh bing Aubergines coated in batter and fried.

Jien dan tsu pai Fried pork chops and stir-fried onions seasoned with chilli pepper and soy.

Jien ga li chio Deep-fried cornmeal clam cakes.

Jien hwang san quai Eels in egg batter deep-fried.

Jien sa tsan yu Marinated smelts in egg batter deep-fried.

Jien tsu ro bing Fried pork meat cakes served with duck sauce.

Jien yu chio Cornmeal fishcakes of flaked flounder, minced shrimps or clams deep-fried.

Jien yu tze Deep-fried shad roe cakes.

Jien yu wei Deep-fried blowfish tails served with Chinese parsley, toasted salt and anise pepper.

Jin chiang ji Boned chicken legs stuffed with ham, steamed, coated with batter and roasted; served sliced in coin shapes.

Jing go bai tsai Reconstituted dried shrimps stir-fried with cabbage.

Jing jeng shr yu Shad steamed with ham, pork fat, mushrooms, bamboo shoots and rice wine.

Jing tsen don bing Sliced hard-boiled eggs stir-fried in flavourful sauce served over lettuce leaves.

Jing tsen gee Fried whole chicken simmered with Chinese mushrooms, cloud ears (fungus vegetable) and lily flowers in soy, ginger and sherry.

Jing tsien sha bing Minced shrimp and pork fat cakes fried and surrounded by stir-fried leafy greens with chicken gravy.

Jing yu Steamed sole with mushrooms, golden needles, dates and ham.

Jiu tsen gee Whole chicken, scallions and ginger steamed in rice wine.

Jiu tzao gee Chicken pieces deep-fried and simmered in ginger-flavoured beer.

Jiu tzow ya Whole duck browned then simmered in beer and soy.

Jook Rice gruel usually flavoured with meat and soy.

Jou szu chao ching chiao Soy-marinated pork slices stir-fried with green pepper strips.

Jou wantze tang Pork meatball soup.

Ju gyok fa sun tong Pigs' feet and peanut soup.

Ju hua ji shun Chicken marinated in wine, fried and served dipped in sesame oil and chilli sauce.

Ju mei fa sun tong Pork tail and peanut soup.

Ju yoke yuan ju shiu tsoi Pork meatballs stir-fried with mushrooms, ginger, cabbage and scallions.

Jwei gee Boiled chicken marinated in sherry or whisky for one to two days, served cut into bite-size pieces.

Ka li ngo yoke tong Curried beef soup with potatoes.

Kan pei liang se chiu Scallops simmered with carrot and cucumber in egg-thickened chicken broth.

Kan pien szu chi tou Green beans, minced pork and shrimp stir-fried and flavoured with preserved vegetables.

Kan shao ming hsia Stir-fried whole shrimps flavoured with ginger, chilli sauce, rice wine and scallions.

Kao rang ji Boned whole chicken stuffed with minced pork, ginger and onion, roasted.

Kao ya Whole duck stuffed with red-in-snow (flavouring vegetable) coated with sauce of soy, sugar and cornstarch and roasted over charcoal, served with hoisin sauce, scallions.

Kao yu Pickerel broiled with ginger, bacon and salted black beans.

Kau yuhk; kou rou Pork belly layered with pickles, onions, ginger, garlic, soy, potatoes and turnips, steamed and turned out like a pudding.

Kay jee ghuy Sausage of pigs' intestines stuffed with diced chicken, ham, mushrooms and bamboo shoots.

Keh chow juh yook; chich chao ju rou Sliced pork and spices braised with egg-plant.

Keh jup chow haah kow Shrimp balls braised with sweet peppers and pulped tomatoes.

Keh tsup har Shelled whole shrimps simmered in sweet and sour tomato sauce.

Kieh tsup ngo yoke Shredded beefsteak served with stir-fried sweet onion and peas in tomato-sherry flavoured sauce.

Kong chi ju bok tsoi Meatballs of minced scallops and pork simmered with celery cabbage and mushrooms.

Kong yu ju tsoi fa tong Minced scallops and pork meatball soup.

Kow cheh tze Egg-plant painted with mixture of peanut butter, garlic and salt and grilled.

Kow ngo pai Marinated boneless top sirloin steak broiled and served with stir-fried green pepper strips.

Kow yu pien Flounder fillets marinated in sauce of soy, ginger and sugar, and barbecued.

Kung bao ding; kung po ghuy deng Quick-fried diced chicken served with soy and chilli sauce.

Kung bao gee ding Diced boned chicken breast slightly coated with flour stir-fried with scallions, roasted peanuts, bamboo shoots, sweet pepper in sauce of sugar, soy and rice wine.

Kung bau ming har Deep-fried prawns simmered in soy and chilli sauce.

Kwangtung chao mi fun Stir-fried transparent noodles topped with shredded pork, mushrooms, bamboo shoots, cabbage strips, scallions flavoured with soy.

Kwangtung la tsoi Mustard green hearts pickled in sweet and sour brine.

Kwangtung leung bon la tsoi Mustard green pickle salad with bean sprouts and shredded jellyfish with sweet and sour dressing.

Kwei fei gee Chicken wings stir-fried with bamboo shoots and mushrooms, and simmered in chicken broth flavoured with ginger, soy, sesame oil, scallions and sherry thickened with cornstarch.

La bai tsai Blanched celery cabbage salad tossed with hot pepper flakes, soy, vinegar, sugar and ginger.

La dow ban jiang yu Sea bass or porgy broiled with spicy bean sauce, ginger and scallions.

La-ee-tzee gai kew Marinated, boned and cubed chicken breast deep-fried and served in a sweet-sour sauce with litchis.

La-ee-tzee op Cantonese roast duck in sweet-sour sauce with litchis.

La-ee-tzee yoke kew Deep-fried pork cubes in sweet-sour sauce with litchis.

La gee sik Diced boned chicken breast stir-fried in sherry-soy sauce served on a bed of braised spinach topped with chopped hot peppers.

La jiao tsao san sih Boned pork chop strips stir-fried and combined with fried egg strips, bean curd strips and sweet or hot peppers in a chicken stock-based sauce.

La jiong dow fu Bean curds in slightly thickened sauce flavoured with soy and preserved horse bean chilli sauce.

La jiu yiang ju yoke Small green peppers stuffed with ground pork flavoured with soy, ginger and simmered in chicken broth.

La jiu yiang ngo yoke Small green peppers stuffed with minced beef flavoured with soy and ginger and simmered in chicken broth.

La tze gee Diced boned chicken breast stir-fried in savoury sauce of hoisin, soy, crushed red-hot pepper and bamboo shoots.

La tze gee ding Boned diced chicken breast stir-fried with sweet and hot pepper, ginger, bamboo shoots served in sweet-sour sauce.

La tze shiao niu ro ding Diced veal cutlet stir-fried with hot pepper served in sweet-sour sauce.

La wei fan Chinese sausage, mushrooms, snow peas and celery cabbage stir-fried with savoury sauce and served over rice.

Lap tsong tsing ju yoke Steamed minced pork and water chestnuts garnished with minced Chinese pork sausage.

Lau yin dun rieh Nest of fried cellophane noodles filled with a mixture of pork, chicken breast, mushrooms, carrot, water chestnut, sliced pineapple, crab meat and blanched almonds in a sweet-sour sauce flavoured with soy, ginger, pineapple juice, sherry; garnished with almonds, popularly called 'Lunar Landing'.

Leen fa tong Chinese mushrooms stuffed with minced pork, bamboo shoots, ginger juice, soy mixture served in chicken broth with leafy vegetables and additional bamboo shoot slices.

Li tze dun ya Duck pieces stir-fried with soy, sugar and sherry then simmered with chestnuts.

Li tze feng A sweet of mashed chestnuts topped with cream.

Liang ban bo tsai Blanched spinach and hickory smoked cheese salad dressed with vinegar, sesame oil and soy.

Liang ban yao pien Pork kidneys boiled and served over blanched cucumber dressed with peanut butter, ginger, vinegar.

Liang bun dung yong tsoi Agar agar salad topped with chicken strips or ham.

Liang bun sub gum Mixed vegetable salad.

Liang pang san szu Vermicelli sheets served with a topping of salted cucumber and shredded chicken or ham.

Lien ngo yoke bang Lotus root, minced pork, preserved kohlrabi, soy formed into flat cakes and pan-fried.

Lo bok gow Turnips boiled in chicken broth mixed with chopped dried shrimp, mushrooms, chopped ham and rice flour and steamed.

Lo han chai Vegetarian chop suey of cellophane noodles and mixed vegetables in chicken broth.

Lo mi gai Whole chicken steamed in mixture of glutinous rice, black mushrooms, bamboo shoots and seasonings.

Lo mi tzu Dumplings of glutinous rice flour filled with sweet bean paste steamed then rolled in coconut flakes.

Lo po pai gu tong Turnip and spare-rib soup.

Loh dow ya tsao ro si Stir-fried bean sprouts with pork.

Loh hon choi; luo han cai An elaborate ensemble of black seaweed, lily flowers, cellophane noodles, gingko nuts, dried mushrooms, bean curd skins, puffy cakes of bean curd, bamboo shoots, green peas, cabbage cooked in broth seasoned with soy and spices, often eaten as a main meal on meatless days.

Lu shun bao yu Abalone, asparagus, cooked turkey breast, mushrooms and ginger stir-fried and blended into chicken broth.

Lu shun dow fu tong Elaborate soup of chicken broth with dried mushrooms, dried shrimp, chicken breast, asparagus and bean curds.

Lu sun tsu ti Pork hocks braised in soy-ginger broth served with asparagus.

Lu zhudu Tripe simmered until fork-tender (chopstick) in broth of ginger, five spices powder, sherry, chicken stock and soy.

Lun ban dow ya Blanched bean sprout salad dressed with vinegar, sugar, sesame oil.

Lun ban fan keh har Tomato and shrimp salad.

Lun ban gee Cold chicken slices served with sauce of peanut oil, sesame oil and soy garnished with scallions.

Lun ban gee si mien Noodles in chicken broth topped with grated carrots, chopped chicken meat and soy, eaten cold.

Lun ban huang gwa Cucumber salad.

Lun ban la chiao dow ya Spicy bean sprout salad.

Lun ban la-ee-tzee ya Litchi nut and roast duck salad.

Lun ban lung shu tsai Asparagus salad.

Lun ban shiao lo bo Sweet and sour cold radishes.

Lun ban tien tsin bai tsai Blanched celery cabbage salad dressed with vinegar, soy, sesame oil.

Lung chwan feng yi tong Soup of boned chicken wings stuffed with ham and bamboo shoots.

Lung ha fu yung Omelette of lobster meat, bamboo shoots, water chestnuts and mushrooms.

Lung ha fun see Stir-fried lobster in shell in elaborate sauce of minced pork, ginger, scallions in soup stock thickened with egg and garnished with fried cellophane noodles.

Lung sha yu mi gung Lobster and sweet corn soup thickened with egg and cornstarch.

Lung shu yen yuen Meatballs of pork, shrimp, water chestnuts, strips of won ton skin in chicken broth.

Ma la tze gee Marinated bite-size pieces of chicken gently fried and served in a sweet-sour sauce.

Ma po dow fu Bean curd braised with thick soy and hot pepper, minced pork and chopped mushrooms.

Ma tie ngo yoke bang Ground beef steamed with water chestnuts, ginger, scallion and soy sauce.

Ma ti tsen tsu ro Minced pork steamed with water chestnuts.

Ma yiou ji; ma yau ghuy Deep-fried chicken chopped and served in sesame oil sauce.

Maih fan jing yuhk; mi fen zheng rou Marinated pork coated with aromatic rice flour and steamed on a bed of sliced potatoes or lotus root.

Maw gwooh chow ghuy pien; mo gu chao ji pian Thinly sliced chicken breast fried with mushrooms and garlic.

Maw gwooh mun baak gup Squabs rubbed with seasoning, layered with ham slices, simmered with mushrooms and served with braised sugar peas.

Mei kwei don gow Steamed cake with fragrant roses.

Meixue zhengchun Baked apple and banana layers in egg custard topped with meringue.

Men yiou tsai Stir-fried cabbage hearts, mushrooms and bamboo shoots.

Mien Generic name for noodles. **Char siu chao** fried noodles with braised Chinese roast pork, cabbage, bamboo shoots and bean sprouts in a rich sauce; **cheung sao** fried noodles with vegetables, chicken and pork shreds; **ching chao** stir-fried plain noodles flavoured with soy; **chung yo** boiled noodles flavoured with simmered dried shrimps, onions and soy; **fun see tsin dan** cellophane noodles steamed with egg and dried shrimp; **fun see niu ro** cellophane noodles with shredded beef; **ha chow** fried noodles with shrimps; **hsia ren chao mi fen** cellophane noodles with celery and prawns; **ieh fooh** Chinese vermicelli stir-fried with pork and tomato; **ja jiang mian** boiled noodles topped with minced pork and mixed vegetables; **jiang bao tsu ro** fried noodles with rich sauce of ground pork, mushrooms flavoured with hoisin, brown bean, soy, ginger and garlic; **liang ban** noodle salad with carrots and lettuce dressed with pickled ginger, soy, vinegar and sesame oil; **lun ban gee se** cold boiled noodles with shredded chicken breast and vegetables; **lun ban ho twei** cold boiled noodles with vegetables and ham; **ma yee song sue** fried cellophane noodles served in spicy, peppery sauce and ground pork or beef; **nung tong** boiled noodles in thick gravy of eggs, mushrooms, wood ears, pork and chicken stock; **shijin chaomian** boiled noodles with shredded pork, fried shredded eggs, bamboo shoots, prawns and spinach leaves moistened with chicken stock and stir-fried to warm; **tiem shwin** fried noodles in sweet-sour sauce; **yuin twei si** boiled noodles with ham and sesame oil.

Mien jing tsao er dung Vegetarian steak with mushrooms, bamboo shoots, cloud ears, lily flowers in slightly thickened sauce.

Mien sie jiong lung ha Chopped lobster in shell stir-fried with garlic and ginger then simmered in slightly thickened chicken broth flavoured with brown bean sauce and soy.

Ming sun kwoh Deep-fried peanuts flavoured with sugar, five spices powder, anise pepper and salt.

Mo er ching do yu pien Flounder fillets stir-fried with wood ears and peas in slightly thickened chicken broth flavoured with soy, sherry and ginger.

Mo gu ji pian Chicken breast slices quick-fried with sugar peas and mushrooms.

Mo gwa tong Hairy melon soup with dried scallops and pork.

Mo shu ro Eggs stir-fried with pork, mushrooms and cloud ears.

Mooi choy jing yook bang; mai tsai jeng rou bing Minced pork steamed with pickled cabbage, water chestnuts and mushrooms.

Muhk seui yuhk; mu shu rou Shredded pork stir-fried with bamboo shoots, wood ears then combined with shredded fried egg flavoured with wine and sesame oil.

Mun keh Aubergine pieces braised with shredded pork flavoured with dried shrimp, ginger and soy sauce.

Mun yu tse Chicken simmered with shark fins, ham, dried scallops and ginger served in cooking broth slightly thickened with chestnut flour.

Mwei jiong gai Bite-size pieces of chicken simmered with celery, ginger, plum sauce, carrots and Chinese pickles served in cooking sauce slightly thickened with cornstarch.

Mwei jiong yoke Boned bite-size pieces of pork simmered with carrots, celery and scallions in plum sauce.

Naahm jin yuhn ji Minced pork formed into balls simmered in flavoured broth.

Nam yu fa shu Peanuts cooked with red bean curd cheese.

Nam yu mun mook yu Squid and pork tenderloin stir-fried in sauce flavoured with red bean cheese and soy.

Nam yu tsu ro Pork butt boiled and then steamed with ginger, sherry and red bean curd cheese served with cooking juices.

Nan gwa niu ro Beef slices steamed with pumpkin.

Nankiang dow fu Fried bean curd simmered with chicken broth, ham, bamboo shoots and soy.

Neuhng dung gu Large Chinese dried mushrooms reconstituted and stuffed with minced pork, garlic, beaten egg and onion simmered in flavoured broth.

Ng heong gai Chicken pieces stir-fried with soy, anise, hoisin sauce, ginger and scallions.

Ng hiong fa sun Peanuts roasted with five spices powder.

Ngaah choy chow haah Shelled chopped shrimps braised with Chinese peas, cloud ears, celery and ginger in slightly thickened soy-flavoured sauce.

Ngaah choy chow juh yook Pork slices braised with pea sprouts, celery, Chinese peas and cloud ears in soy-flavoured sauce.

Ngh lauh yuh Whole steamed, poached or fried fish in sweet-sour sauce made piquant with addition of pickled vegetables such as ginger, cucumber, turnip, chilli and mushrooms—a party dish usually referred to as 'Five Willow Fish'.

Ngo maih faahn Savoury rice with Chinese roast pork or soy-braised chicken tightly wrapped in lotus leaf and steamed.

Ngo pa kew Beef steak braised with snow peas and Chinese mushrooms flavoured with oyster and soy sauce, ginger, garlic and scallion, served in cooking juice slightly thickened with cornstarch.

Ngo yoke lo mien Steak and noodles with shredded carrots, celery and bean sprouts in soy and ginger sauce.

Ngo yoke yuen fun see tong Beef meatball soup with cellophane noodles.

Ngo yoke yuen shiu tsoi tong Beef meatball and cellophane noodle soup with celery cabbage.

Ngung faah yook mun sun Flavoured pork strips stir-fried with salted dried bamboo shoots.

Ning er tsao tsu gahn Pork liver stir-fried with peas and cloud ears.

Ning mong pi tsao hai Cracked crab in shell stir-fried in black bean, lemon and ginger, then simmered in slightly thickened chicken broth flavoured with soy, sugar and rice wine.

Ning mung bun gum chong yu Tuna fish salad with bean sprouts dressed with lemon juice, ginger and scallions.

Ning mung gook gai Chicken pieces covered with lemon juice and honey coated in flour and baked.

Niu nao tsao gee don Eggs stir-fried with calf brains.

Niu ro Generic name for stir-fried beef. **Bai tsai** stir-fried with Chinese cabbage, spinach or celery cabbage; **ching** stir-fried with green peas; **ching jiao tsao** stir-fried with green peppers; **ching tsai** stir-fried with celery; **dung gu** stir-fried with black mushrooms; **dung sun** stir-fried with bamboo shoots; **gai lan** stir-fried with mustard greens or broccoli; **ho yow tsao ngo yoke** stir-fried with oyster sauce; **hwa tsai** stir-fried with cauliflower; **sheh do** stir-fried with snow peas; **tsao ching tsai** stir-fried with carrots, peas, mushrooms and peppers; **tsao fan chieh** stir-fried with tomatoes; **tsao gu** stir-fried with fresh mushrooms; **tza tsai** stir-fried with kohlrabi; **yang tsung** stir-fried with onions.

Niu ro ching do Ground beef and peas flavoured with soy.

Niu ro loh do ya Beef slices braised in sauce to which is added bean sprouts the last minute of cooking.

Niu ro tsao fan Roast beef and fried rice garnished with egg strips and peas.

Niu ro tsen dow fu Shredded beef steamed with bean curds in soy and rice wine.

Noh mai gai guen Glutinous rice, chopped chicken breast, Chinese sausages, mushrooms, dried shrimp and ham formed into rolls and baked.

Noh mai ju yoke gai Chicken stuffed with pork and glutinous rice, black mushrooms and bamboo shoots, simmered in broth.

Nying ya ro si Shredded pork stir-fried with bean sprouts and scallions.

Pai gu mun yu Simmered spare-ribs, bass and turnips served with a sauce of ginger, scallions, soy, vinegar and sesame oil.

Pai gwut lo bo tong Turnip and spare-rib soup.

Pang pang chi Cellophane noodles served with shredded chicken and paper-thin cucumber slices in broth.

Pay daahn 'Hundred-year-old eggs' – duck eggs preserved in tea leaves, lime ash and pine shavings left to mature for about three months; eaten sliced as is or used as a garnish in vegetable and meat dishes.

Pow tsai Hot Chinese cabbage pickles.

Quncai ban zhengan Chicken gizzards and celery salad dressed with soy, vinegar and sesame oil.

Quingdou xiaren Stir-fried prawns and peas in sherry, ginger and soy sauce.

Rahng chieh tze Aubergine halves stuffed with flavoured ground pork, water chestnuts, ginger and scallions steamed in chicken broth.

Ring tzei gee pien Boned diced chicken breasts, ham, Chinese mushrooms, bamboo shoots, scallions, ginger stir-fried and served in soy-rice wine sauce.

Ro guen bo tsai Flavoured pork filling in egg skins served over a bed of spinach braised in chicken broth.

Ro pien lo bo tong Pork and turnip soup.

Ro sih dow fu Sliced or ground pork stir-fried and simmered with bean curd in soup broth flavoured with soy, gin, wine, ginger, garlic and sugar.

Ro sih fun see Sliced pork stir-fried in soy-flavoured sauce and simmered with cellophane noodles, mushrooms and water chestnuts.

Ro si lo mien Stir-fried ground pork, cabbage, mushrooms simmered in chicken broth served over noodles.

Ro si tong Pork slivers, mushrooms and bamboo shoots in chicken broth.

Ro sung Pork loin slow-cooked in chicken broth until meat disintegrates into sauce to become a lumpy mixture to be served hot or cold.

Ro yuen tong Pork and shrimp meatballs in pork broth.

Ru ee fu yong don Plain egg fu yong with bean sprouts, mushrooms, water chestnuts.

Ru koh Squab braised in chicken broth flavoured with anise, cinnamon, sherry, soy and sugar.

Ru ee tza gee Chicken pieces marinated in soy, deep-fried.

Ruan dza go jiu Chopped dates, raisins and apricots mixed with peanut butter, sesame seeds, egg whites and deep-fried.

Sa go lung sha Lobster meat mixed with scallions, eggs, chicken broth, garlic and cornstarch baked in casserole.

Sa go shia ro Crab meat in casserole with egg-thickened chicken broth.

Sa wo baahk yuhk Red-cooked pork (simmered in soy-broth) cut into chunks and placed in casserole with wine, sliced bamboo shoots, mushrooms, Chinese cabbage, scallions and ginger root to simmer.

Sa wo yuh chi; sha guo yu chi Shark's fin cooked in casserole with ham, bamboo shoots, shredded dried mushrooms with chicken broth and rice wine with addition of celery cabbage just before serving.

Sa yang ro A large fondue fish of chicken broth in which diners cook pieces of thinly sliced lamb and vegetables such as spinach, celery cabbage, bean curds and cellophane noodles; the cooked foods are then dipped into sauces of ginger-vinegar, soy-sesame seed, peanut butter, minced scallions, ginger, etc.

Sai hung chih wohng huhn ngauh yuhk Partially cooked red-cooked meat fried in oil to which tomatoes are added; the gravy is flavoured with chilli sauce.

Sai kun sin yau Quick-fried squid with celery.

Sam di dow fu Fried bean curds stir-fried with Chinese mushrooms, bamboo shoots, ginger and garlic simmered in sauce of soy, sugar and sherry.

Sang bau yihm jin yuhk Pork slices shallow-fried with black beans, chilli pepper, soy and rice wine.

Sang tsoi bao yoke bang Minced pork stir-fried with water chestnuts and lettuce leaves in slightly thickened sauce of soup stock, soy and sugar.

San pu chan Fried pudding of eggs, cornflour and sugar.

Sao niu pa Marinated steak broiled.

Sao yo yu gee Reconstituted dried squid stir-fried with chicken pieces, ginger and soy simmered with Chinese mushrooms and bamboo shoots.

Sar wor yu tau Fish heads, bamboo shoots, bean curds and mushrooms stewed in soy.

See jew ghuy peen Quick-fried sliced chicken and vegetables in chilli and black bean sauce.

Sha guan Shrimp-filled egg skins simmered in chicken broth garnished with shredded ham.

Sha guan fun see Shrimp rolls simmered in broth with chopped Chinese cabbage and cellophane noodles.

Sha hwang si tze tou Meatballs of pork and crab meat fried then simmered in chicken broth with celery cabbage.

Sha hwang yu du Fish maws simmered in ginger-flavoured chicken broth served with sauce of crab meat, sugar, sherry and soy slightly thickened with cornstarch.

Sha mi bo tsai nee Stir-fried spinach flavoured with dried shrimp.

Sha mi sao lo bo Reconstituted dried shrimps simmered in chicken broth with turnips.

Sha mi tsao don Scrambled eggs with dried shrimp.

Sha mi tzu gahn si Shredded bean curd simmered in chicken broth with dried shrimp, Chinese mushrooms, ginger.

Sha ren ching do Shrimp stir-fried with peas.

Sha ren dow fu Shrimp stir-fried with bean curd.

Sha ro bai tsai Crab meat stir-fried with ginger and scallions in sherry served on a bed of celery cabbage braised in broth.

Sha ro hung lo bo Spare-ribs simmered in chicken broth with shredded carrots and combined with fresh crab meat, ginger and sherry to simmer in the slightly thickened sauce.

Sha tze go te dow fu Marinated bean curd deep-fried and layered with shrimps and steamed in chicken broth.

Sha tze ro chio Shrimps steamed with pork, water chestnuts, ginger and soy.

Sha yuen Shrimp and water chestnut balls cooked in boiling water served with duck sauce.

Shang sue bai ko Deep-fried squid covered with mixture of mushrooms, chestnuts, raisins, gingko nuts and kohlrabi simmered with ginger, soy, sugar, sherry and soup stock.

Shang tsong fan Steamed Chinese sausage served over rice.

Shen hsien jou Boned belly pork steamed in sherry and soy.

Shia tze lo han chai Shrimp stir-fried with mixed Chinese vegetables served in a sauce of beef broth, sherry and soy.

Shiao niu nao ban dow fu Calf brain stir-fried with ham, bamboo shoots, mushrooms and ginger simmered in broth and soy.

Shigwa tsen gee Diced chicken mixed with bamboo shoots, ham, eggs, sherry and ginger placed in hollow water-melon and steamed until melon is tender.

Shieh do ro pien Stir-fried sliced pork with bamboo shoots, mushrooms and snow peas.

Shieh li Red-in-snow–a vegetable much used in Chinese cooking, the dried or canned variety used as a flavouring in many dishes such as the following: **hung ro si** with pork; **tsai ro si hu lo bo** with pork and carrots; **tsai tsao shiao niu ro si** with veal; **tsai niu ro si** with beef; **tsai ro si fan** with pork and rice.

Shien dan tsen ro bing Minced pork steamed with water chestnuts and salted duck egg.

Shien gu niu nao Calf brain stir-fried with ham, bamboo shoots, mushrooms and ginger simmered in chicken broth and soy.

Shihtze tou Meatballs of pork, shrimp and mushroom.

Shijin chaofan Elaborate fried rice with mushrooms, prawns, ham, pork, bamboo shoots, peas and fried egg strips.

Shijin chaomian Elaborate fried noodle dish of pork, bamboo shoots, prawns and green vegetables in chicken stock garnished with fried egg strips.

Shing jen ya Marinated duck steamed and boned layered with mixture of peas, almonds, water chestnuts and eggs and cooked in oven.

Shing ren ching do Green beans stir-fried and garnished with sliced almonds.

Shing ren lu shun Stir-fried asparagus garnished with sliced almonds.

Shu tzai nam yu yoke Boiled pork pieces and potatoes in broth flavoured with red bean curd cheese and soy.

Shueh tsai mao dow ro si Shredded pork stir-fried with green beans and bamboo shoots.

Shuin don Marinated hard-boiled eggs smoked in brown sugar and tea leaves to lend a smoky flavour to them.

Shuin tow dhan dow Green beans stir-fried with garlic.

Shwe tsai li yu Whole fish simmered in sherry, chicken broth and sliced bamboo shoots flavoured with red-in-snow (vegetable fungus flavouring).

Shwin gee Whole chicken stuffed with scallions and steamed over brown sugar to lend a smoky flavour.

Shwin la ju hiok Pigs' feet simmered in hot pepper and ginger-flavoured broth.

Shwintow dow si yu Boiled whole fish served with stir-fried bamboo shoots, Chinese mushrooms and scallions in sauce flavoured with black beans, garlic, soy, ginger.

Shwin yu Whole carp marinated in ginger, sherry, five spices powder, soy and sugar and deep-fried.

Si tsup ngo ba yip Beef tripe fried in ginger, onion and garlic and simmered in soy and catsup broth until tender.

Si yow gai Whole chicken quick-boiled in soy and brown sugar served cut into bite-size pieces.

Sien ha mi fun Stir-fried shrimps, mushrooms, bamboo shoots and Chinese cabbage mixed with rice sticks flavoured with soy and garlic.

Sien tsai tsao yo yu Reconstituted dried squid stir-fried in seasonings and simmered in meat stock with pickled mustard greens and bamboo shoots.

Sieu ghuy Grilled whole chicken basted with soy, sugar, garlic and Chinese spices.

31

Sieu juh Roast loin of pork basted with sugar, honey and Chinese spices.

Sieu ngaap Roast whole duck basted with honey, soy and Chinese spices.

Sih tze do Pork meatballs steamed on layer of stir-fried celery cabbage leaves.

Siu ju gyok Pigs' feet simmered in ginger, soy, garlic and sugar broth.

Siu ngauh taih gan Boiled calves' feet cut into strips and stir-fried with cabbage, French beans, asparagus tips, eaten as much for its firm, jelly-like sauce, as for the meat.

So jap kum Fried mixed vegetables.

Soo tsao wong san Eel coated in egg batter and fried.

Soong yoke Minced pork stir-fried with bamboo shoots, water chestnuts and snow peas covered with chicken broth flavoured with soy and oyster sauce served with a mound of fried cellophane noodles on top.

Sou sahp gam; su shi jin Stir-fried mixture of Chinese mushrooms, shredded carrots, bamboo shoots, cabbage, wood ears, cucumber and bean sprouts flavoured with soy and wine.

Sue ho twei dow fu Dried bean curd sheets reconstituted in soy-water layered with bean curd skins and steamed.

Sue sao ya Stir-fried bamboo shoots and mushrooms placed in alternating layers with bean curds coated with flavouring mixture, first steamed and then deep-fried; commonly referred to as Vegetarian Roast Duck.

Suen la bai tsoi Parboiled celery cabbage dressed with mustard, soy and vinegar.

Sun pien tsao tsu gahn Pork liver strips marinated in sherry and cornstarch and stir-fried, combined with stir-fried bamboo shoots served in slightly thickened sauce.

Sun sih tsai shing Stir-fried Chinese cabbage and bamboo shoots in a lightly flavoured chicken broth sauce.

Sun tsai shiao niu ro pien Marinated veal cutlets stir-fried with soy and rice wine served with stir-fried lettuce.

Sung ji tsu Shredded chicken breasts quick-fried with chillis, covered with pine kernels and served with lettuce leaves which are used for wrapping the pieces in.

Swan la ti pong Fresh boiled ham cut in pieces fried with hot peppers and ginger and reheated in chicken broth flavoured with vinegar and sugar.

Swan la tsai Stir-fried celery cabbage with hot and sour dressing.

Swan tsai ban sha mi Preserved mustard greens and bamboo shoots mixed with reconstituted dried shrimps served dressed with sesame oil, vinegar and soy sauce.

Swan tsai tsen pai gu Spare-ribs steamed with brown bean sauce and pickled mustard greens.

Syut choi chaau ha yahn Prawns stir-fried with ginger, garlic and chopped snow pickles.

Szutu yu Whole sea bass steamed and served bathed in sauce of scallions, ginger, garlic, soy and rice wine.

Ta sih mi Lamb slices marinated in sugar and brown bean sauce, stir-fried then simmered in sweet-sour sauce.

Tang tsu yu Shanghai-style bass or porgy lightly coated in batter, deep-fried until crispy, served in sweet-sour sauce garnished with shrimp and peas.

Tangcu liyu Whole carp deep-fried and served in a sweet-sour sauce with water chestnuts, bamboo shoots and green peppers.

Tao jen jiang tze ro Boned pork cubes stir-fried with almonds and sugar, simmered in sauce of soy, ginger and beer.

Tiem shwin api gwut   Spare-ribs coated in batter, deep-fried then simmered in sweet-sour sauce with pineapples, tomatoes and green pepper strips.

Tiem shwin gai gon   Marinated chicken livers served with stir-fried cucumbers in sweet-sour sauce.

Tiem shwin gai jap   Chicken giblets in sweet-sour sauce.

Tiem shwin kong yu-chu   Marinated scallops coated in batter and deep-fried served in sweet-sour sauce with green pepper strips and pineapple chunks.

Tiem shwin mien   Boiled noodles stir-fried in sweet-sour sauce.

Tiem swan bai tsai   Cabbage in sweet-sour sauce.

Tiem sween la chiu yu   Canton-style fried fish in sweet-sour sauce flavoured with sweet and hot peppers.

Tien gee mun kow fu   Frogs' legs marinated and coated in batter stir-fried with Chinese vegetarian steak (meat substitute made of wheat gluten) simmered in chicken broth with soy.

Tien gee tsao ching do   Shanghai-style frogs' legs stir-fried with peas.

Tien swan gee jiu   Boned chicken pieces marinated in honey and lemon juice, coated with batter and deep-fried served in a sweet-sour sauce.

Tien swan hwang gwa   Stir-fried cucumbers in sweet-sour sauce.

Tien swan jiang se gee   Simmered chicken cut into bite-size pieces served in a sauce of ginger, vinegar, sugar and sesame.

Tien swan pong sha   Cracked crabs coated in batter, deep-fried and served in a sweet-sour sauce.

Tien swan ro jieu   Beef meatballs in sweet-sour sauce with pineapple chunks, sweet pickles, tomato and green pepper.

Tien swan ro jiu   Steamed pork cubes coated with batter, deep-fried and simmered in sweet and pungent sauce with pineapple and green pepper strips.

Tien swan sha   Stir-fried large, whole shrimp served in sweet-sour sauce flavoured with tomato paste.

Tien swan sue ro jiu   Walnut halves coated in batter, deep-fried combined with stir-fried sweet red and green peppers in sweet-sour sauce; referred to as Vegetarian Meatballs.

Tien swan yo yu   Shanghai-style reconstituted dried squid stir-fried and combined with stir-fried wood ears, bamboo shoots in slightly thickened sweet-sour sauce.

Tien swan yu   Whole baked sea bass with stir-fried carrots, onions and sweet pickles in sweet-sour sauce.

Tien swan yu tiao   Fish sticks in sweet-sour sauce.

Tien tsin bai tsai gee tong   Chicken soup with celery cabbage and cellophane noodles.

Tihm syun ap; tian suan ya   Pre-cooked duck slices coated in flour and beaten duck egg and shallow-fried until crisp served in a sweet-sour sauce.

Tit wo daan; tie guo dan   Chinese soufflé of eggs, minced pork, soy and lard.

Tjo bang   Prune pancakes served as a dessert.

Tohng jing yuhk; tang zheng rou   Marinated pork belly steamed with brown sugar until meat turns into consistency of jelly.

Tou ku cheng yu   Cantonese-style steamed fish in black bean sauce, ginger and rice wine.

Tou sha   Sweet red bean paste used as a filling in steamed dumplings.

Tou shih hsiang ku kua   Bitter melons stuffed with pork and shrimp mixture in black bean sauce.

Tsai gahn bei ding Fresh scallops stir-fried with Chinese mushrooms, water chestnuts, bamboo shoots and Chinese spices.

Tsan do sha ren Shanghai-style shrimp stir-fried with baby lima beans, asparagus, ginger and scallions served in a heavy sauce of chicken broth, sherry and soy thickened with corn-flour.

Tsao bao yu Abalone stir-fried with Chinese mushrooms, ginger, scallions, celery cabbage and bamboo shoots.

Tsao da sha Shrimp braised with water chestnuts, mush-rooms, ham and peas served in a slightly thickened sauce of chicken broth, soy and sherry.

Tsao gai lan Chinese broccoli stir-fried with wine and ginger.

Tsao gee gahn Chicken livers marinated in gin stir-fried with bamboo shoots, water chestnuts and simmered in stock.

Tsao gu niu ro Marinated beef slices stir-fried with mush-rooms.

Tsao gu tsen gee Cornish hen cut into bite-size pieces steamed with mushrooms, ginger, scallions and soy.

Tsao ku pa tsai tan Stir-fried lettuce with straw mush-rooms.

Tsao liu yu pien Peking-style fish slices simmered with wood ears and scallions in rice wine and chicken broth.

Tsao lung ha Cracked lobster in shell served in an elaborate sauce of minced pork, black beans and soy in soup stock thickened with beaten eggs; commonly referred to as Lobster Cantonese.

Tsao mo yu Fresh squid stir-fried with minced pork, mushrooms and bamboo shoots then simmered in chicken broth, soy, vinegar and sesame oil.

Tsao sam sic Stir-fried red and green peppers combined with stir-fried marinated chicken breast shreds simmered in brown bean sauce.

Tsao sha jiu Shrimp nuggets coated in batter, deep-fried and served in peppery hot sweet-sour sauce.

Tsao san hu Eels stir-fried with ginger, flavoured with sesame.

Tsao sha yao Stir-fried kidneys, shrimps, water chestnuts and snow pea pods flavoured with ginger, soy and scallions.

Tsao shiao niu ro pien Stir-fried veal slices combined with stir-fried celery, Chinese mushrooms, celery cabbage in a light sauce.

Tsao sih jing Stir-fried pork pieces, diced ham and chicken wings simmered in chicken broth with mushrooms and bamboo shoots.

Tsao sue pong sha ro Mashed carrot and mashed potato stir-fried until crisp then combined with shredded bamboo shoots, Chinese mushrooms and snow peas flavoured with wine; commonly called Vegetarian Stir-fried Crab Meat.

Tsao sue yu pien Stir-fried wood ears and snow peas combined in light sauce with deep-fried potatoes; commonly called Vegetarian Stir-fried Sliced Fish.

Tsao tien gee twei Szechuan-style frogs' legs stir-fried with sweet and hot peppers simmered in chicken broth flavoured with hoisin and soy sauce.

Tsao tsu gahn Pork liver stir-fried with Chinese mushrooms and bamboo shoots then simmered in flavoured broth.

Tsao yah gahn Duck livers stir-fried with Chinese mush-rooms and shredded bamboo shoots and simmered in chicken broth, soy and sherry.

Tsao yang ro Shredded lamb stir-fried with onion, bamboo shoots, water chestnuts and snow peas served topped with deep-fried cellophane noodles.

Tsao yao hwa Pork kidneys stir-fried with cloud ears and bamboo shoots.

Tsao yow yu Cantonese-style reconstituted dried squid stir-fried in rice wine, ginger and soy then combined with stir-fried cloud ears and water chestnuts.

Tsao yu pien Haddock strips stir-fried with mushrooms, celery, snow peas, ginger and scallions served in broth-soy sauce.

Tse jiang tsao ya pien Boned duck slices stir-fried with spring ginger and simmered in sherry and soy broth.

Tse jiang ya pien Szechuan-style pickled ginger duck— boned breast of duck stir-fried with ginger and simmered in sauce of chicken broth, brown bean sauce, pickled peppers and green peppers, served with Chinese hot sauce.

Tsen ba bao yah Shanghai-style whole duck stuffed with shrimp, mushrooms, peanuts, barley, ground pork, fresh scallops and glutinous rice seasoned with soy and spices and steamed; commonly called Eight Precious Duck.

Tsen bai tsai Celery cabbage steamed with chopped dried shrimps.

Tsen chieh nee Steamed aubergine slices served with sesame oil.

Tsen do chieh tze Aubergine slices stir-fried, combined with stir-fried lima beans and simmered in pork and ginger sauce.

Tsen pong sha Steamed crabs coated with sauce of ginger, soy, vinegar.

Tsen ro jiu Meatballs of ground pork, black mushrooms, water chestnuts and condiments, steamed.

Tsen sih yu Whole shad stuffed with scallions and steamed with shredded ham, ginger, sherry, vinegar and soy.

Tsen tsu ro Pork slices steamed in sauce of brown beans, sugar, ginger, scallions and rice flour.

Tsen tsu ro chiu Pork meatballs coated with glutinous rice and steamed.

Tsen yu Fresh whole fish steamed with salted black beans, sherry, soy and ginger.

Tsing heong chong gai Chicken pieces layered with Chinese sausages and mushrooms, steamed with soy and sesame oil.

Tsing la–ee–tzee fo twei Ham steamed with litchi nuts.

Tsing lung ha yoke bang Bite-size pieces of unshelled lobster steamed in sauce of minced pork, water chestnuts, soy, ginger.

Tsow mun gai Whole chicken simmered in broth of sherry, ginger, soy and garlic, cut into bite-size pieces and served with thickened cooking liquid.

Tsu ro lo mien Elaborate dish of pork, shredded cabbage, bamboo shoots, celery, mushrooms and snow peas cooked in flavoured broth and served poured over fried noodles.

Tsu ro mun li tze Boned pork slow-cooked in soy broth with chestnuts.

Tsu ro sao er dung Pork butt stewed with mushrooms and bamboo shoots.

Tsu ro tsao gai tsai Stir-fried pork slices with green peppers in broth and soy gravy.

Tsu ro tsao hwa tsai Stir-fried pork with cauliflower.

Tsu ro tsao yang tsung Stir-fried pork with onions.

Tsu suh sao sun pien Braised pork tongue with bamboo shoots.

Tsu yu pien Red snapper or sea bass fillets simmered in chicken broth flavoured with ginger and scallions served in sherry-soy sauce garnished with Chinese parsley.

Tsung fa dow fu Fresh bean curd salad dressed with oil, salt and scallions.

Tsung fa tsen don Steamed egg custard with scallions and soy.

Tsung hwa don Scrambled eggs with scallions.

Tsung pao yang jou Mutton slices stir-fried with scallions served in broth and soy sauce.

Tsung shang yu Whole fish simmered with scallions and served in a slightly thickened sauce of ginger, garlic, soy and sugar.

Tsung tsen gee Whole chicken stuffed with ginger and scallions, steamed with sherry.

Tswei pi gee Cornish hen stuffed with ginger and scallions, simmered in seasoned broth then deep-fried and served with pineapple rings and maraschino cherries.

Tswei pi ya Shanghai-style whole duck marinated in ginger, garlic, soy, anise pepper and rice wine steamed then deep-fried.

Tung gu pa ya Duck split open, deep-fried and steamed with ginger and scallions served with stir-fried Chinese mushrooms.

Twei pi dza gee Boned chicken nuggets coated in batter and fried with hot sauce or red pepper, then simmered with bamboo shoots and mushrooms in sweet-sour sauce.

Tza ba quai Peking-style marinated chicken pieces deep-fried.

Tza fun see Deep-fried cellophane noodles served as a base or topping for meat and vegetable dishes.

Tza fung wei sha Jumbo shrimps marinated and coated in batter and deep-fried.

Tza gai Cantonese-style fried chicken pieces simmered in gravy of sherry and chicken broth with addition of mushrooms and peas.

Tza gee tzen Boiled chicken gizzards deep-fried and served in sauce of sherry, vinegar and sesame oil.

Tza gu go ba tong Fresh mushrooms and shredded pork simmered in chicken broth served garnished with crackling rice patties.

Tza heh tao Walnuts coated with sugar paste, deep-fried.

Tza kong yu-chu Marinated fresh scallops coated in chestnut flour batter, deep-fried.

Tza ling juh gee Squid coated in light batter, deep-fried.

Tza nahn gwa Pumpkin sticks coated in batter, deep-fried.

Tza ngo ba yip Marinated beef tripe steamed then deep-fried.

Tza pi don Fried 'hundred-year-old eggs' (preserved eggs).

Tza sha Shrimp coated in batter, deep-fried.

Tza sha yuen Shrimp and pork minced, shaped into balls, deep-fried and served on a bed of lettuce.

Tza sun ho kew Fresh oysters coated in batter, deep-fried.

Tza tsoi gee pien tong Preserved kohlrabi, bamboo shoots in chicken broth garnished with chicken breast slices.

Tza tsoi ro si tong Soup of preserved kohlrabi and pork with cellophane noodles.

Tze bao gee Boned chicken breast cubes marinated in sauce, wrapped in paper and deep-fried.

Tze bao ngo pa Marinated steak cubes wrapped in paper with scallions, deep-fried.

Tze bao niu ro Marinated steak cubes, wrapped in paper, steamed.

Tze bao shiao niu Marinated veal cutlet slices wrapped in paper, deep-fried.

Tze fung gee Cubed, boned chicken breasts layered with Chinese mushrooms and thinly-sliced Virginia ham, steamed with sherry and ginger.

Tzing don Beaten eggs steamed with dried shrimps, Chinese mushrooms and ground pork flavoured with ginger and sherry.

Tzu ro si tza tsai Shredded pork stir-fried with shredded preserved kohlrabi and bamboo shoots.

Tzu suh tong Soup of braised pork tongue with bamboo shoots and bean curds.

Waaht ghuy Marinated chicken simmered with golden needles, wood ears and Chinese mushrooms in soy and sherry.

Wan tou chiang Deep-fried marinated pork slices served with peas in soy-sherry sauce.

Wan tou huang Dried peas cooked and pulverized, mixed with sugar, chilled and cut into cubes eaten as a tea snack.

Wang pao chi Whole chicken marinated in condiments and glutinous rice covered in net-like fat, roasted with mushrooms and ham.

Wei go ba Elaborate party dish of marinated boned, diced chicken breast, lobster meat, roast duck, roast pork, shrimp, Chinese mushrooms, bamboo shoots and water chestnuts stir-fried and then simmered in chicken broth, soy, vinegar and sugar, served over crispy rice patties which sizzle upon contact with mixture.

Wei yang ro Shanghai-style leg of boned lamb simmered in spicy broth of ginger, cinnamon, sherry, soy and sugar served with thickened cooking broth.

Wo mien; wo mian Basic pot-cooked noodles different from Chow Mien in that the noodles are par-boiled and not deep-fried and cooked in sauce so that they are softer and more flavourful since they take on the cooking flavours of the garnish.

Won ton hai sun Chinese ravioli soup with sea cucumbers, bamboo shoots and Chinese mushrooms.

Won twei tsen gai Marinated bite-size pieces of chicken steamed with bamboo shoots, mushrooms and Virginia ham.

Wong gwa hoi git pey Jellyfish and cucumber salad dressed with vinegar, sugar and sesame oil.

Wong yo tsen yu Whole bass steamed in hot, spicy sauce of red pepper, black beans, sugar and soy.

Woo siang shwin gee Whole chicken stuffed with scallions, steamed then smoked in cinnamon, molasses and anise, served with hot sauce of pepper, soy and sesame oil.

Woo siang tsen gahn Chicken gizzards stir-fried in spicy sauce then simmered in chicken broth.

Woon dow chow daahn Eggs scrambled with ham, bacon and peas.

Wu hsiang tou Fresh broad beans cooked in broth seasoned with hot pepper and aniseed.

Wu hwa niu ro hwang dow ya tong Beef shank and bean sprout soup.

Wu liu yu Steamed whole fish served with sweet-sour sauce.

Wu se su tsai Vegetable platter of asparagus, carrots, straw mushrooms, baby corn and tomatoes dressed with wine and sesame oil.

Wu shiang gee yeh Chicken wings stir-fried in spicy sauce.

Wu shiang ju gee Cornish hen marinated in five-spice powder, deep-fried.

Wu shiang koh tze Pigeon marinated in five-spice powder and soy, deep-fried, served with toasted salt and anise pepper.

Xi hong shi huang men hiu rou Beef slices braised with tomato.

Xian dan Duck eggs salted in brine for 30–40 days, eaten as is, steamed or used as garnish in meat and vegetable dishes.

Xiaran shao doufu Stir-fried bean curd and prawns in light soy and sherry sauce.

Xie huang yu chi Shark's fin simmered in stock with addition of crab meat and crab eggs, rice wine and lard.

Xierou chao dan Crab omelette served on shredded lettuce.

Xue cai chao xia ren Prawns stir-fried with ginger and garlic with addition of snow pickles (sour and salty condiment).

Xuedo niurou Stir-fried snow peas and marinated steak slices in light sauce flavoured with sherry and oyster sauce.

Ya gahn tong Duck liver soup with bamboo shoots and cabbage.

Yah goh gee ding Boned chicken breast cubes stir-fried in hoisin, soy and sherry garnished with cashew nuts or almonds.

Yang chow haah kow Minced shrimp and fat pork balls deep-fried until puffy and golden.

Yang chow see jee tao Pork and crab meatballs simmered in broth to which is added mushrooms, bamboo shoots and cabbage.

Yang chow tsao er dung Mushrooms and bamboo shoots stir-fried then simmered in chicken broth flavoured with soy, ginger, sherry.

Yang chung kow ju Flounder fillets buried in sliced onions, bathed in sherry and soy and baked.

Yang gow Leg of lamb cooked in soy-flavoured broth until meat shreds, then mixed with cooking liquid and left to gel in refrigerator; eaten as an appetiser.

Yang pai hwang gwa tong Lamb chop and cucumber soup.

Yang ro gai lan Lamb slices stir-fried with broccoli.

Yang tsung mun niu gan Marinated beef liver braised with onion and celery.

Yang tsung niu ro Steak strips quick-cooked in stir-fried bed of onions, ginger, garlic and soy.

Yang tsung pai ku Beef slices stir-fried with green peppers, onions, tomatoes, mushrooms and snow peas.

Yang tsung ro si don kiao Egg omelette with pork, onion and peas.

Yang tsung tsu pai Spare-ribs and onions simmered in sweet-sour sauce.

Yang yu hung sao ya Duck slow-cooked in broth with potatoes.

Yashao ya Duckling simmered in orange juice, soy, ginger root, five-spice powder and chicken stock, then deep-fried and served with reduced cooking liquid.

Yat ban wo; yi pin guo Elaborate hot-pot similar to Peking hot-pot; ingredients are usually pre-cooked chicken, duck, uncooked ham, fried bean curd, fish balls, egg skins stuffed with minced meat, abalone, celery cabbage, pea-starch noodles, dried mushrooms and hardboiled eggs, all of which surround a large simmering pot of chicken stock in which diners dip their selection of food items.

Yeh jiong ga li har Shrimp curry with bamboo shoots in sauce thickened with coconut flakes.

Yem gook gai Whole chicken marinated in seasonings then cooked in a bed of coarse salt.

Yen fung gee Whole chicken cured in salt, then steamed with ginger and scallions.

Yen ju gee   Peking-style chicken placed in deep bed of coarse salt, roasted and served with ginger oil.

Yen lo bo   White turnip pickles.

Yen lo bo si   Sweet-sour white turnip pickles.

Yen swei ya   Duck rubbed with salt, left to cure overnight, then steamed.

Yeong mo gwa   Hairy melon stuffed with minced pork, mushrooms and dried shrimps, steamed.

Yet op liang mei   Duck slow-cooked in soy broth, then boned, shredded and served with grapes seasoned with sesame oil and soy.

Yeung gou; yang guo   Meat of slow-cooked lamb scraped and cooked in its own juice with wine and scallions, gelled and eaten as an appetiser or as garnish for rice congee or noodles.

Yeung gwaah   Braised squash filled with minced fish.

Yeung yu   Minced fish, shrimps, mushrooms, water chestnuts, ham and condiments layered into fish skins and browned in oil.

Yihm wo gai   Chicken hung overnight, buried in salt, baked producing tender, crispy skin and juicy flavourful meat; saltiness does not penetrate beyond the skin.

Yinxiang bao ji   Marinated chicken cubes wrapped with scallions in foil paper and deep-fried.

Yiong gai yik   Boned chicken wings stuffed with minced mushrooms, bamboo shoots and ham, steamed and served with cooking liquid gravy.

Yo bao sha   Shrimp in shell stir-fried in sauce of soy, sugar, sherry, vinegar and ginger until shells are coated with flavouring.

Yo ling gee   Shanghai-style chicken rubbed with seasoning, steamed then deep-fried.

Yo ling ru go   Squab marinated in soy, sherry and ginger, steamed and served with sesame oil.

Yo mun shiao sha   Soft-shell crabs stuffed with ginger, braised in chicken broth, soy and sugar.

Yo twa gee   Peking-style fried chicken – coated with cornstarch and deep-fried.

Yoke yuan shiu tsoi tong   Pork meatball soup with cabbage.

Yong chung ju pai   Marinated pork chops fried then simmered with onion rings.

Yong chung ju pai fun see   Pork chops and onions simmered in chicken broth served with cellophane noodles.

Yong chung ju pai gwut   Pork chops coated with flour browned in fat then simmered in hot and spicy sauce.

Yong chung ju pai mien   Pork chops simmered with onions served in chicken broth with boiled noodles.

Yong dow fu   Fresh bean curds stuffed with minced pork, dried shrimps and condiments, fried and then simmered in chicken broth.

Yong tsung ju gohn   Pork liver and onions stir-fried and served in soy, sherry, sugar and garlic sauce.

Youbao xianxia   Marinated shrimps or prawns in shell, deep-fried.

Youlin ji   Chicken submerged in boiling water, marinated in soy and sherry, deep-fried and served with sauce of ginger, soy, vinegar and yellow beans.

Yow tza bok gop   Squab marinated in ginger, celery, soy and sherry, deep-fried.

Yow tza fa sun   Peanuts deep-fried with onion and garlic.

Yu bing   Fish fillets mixed with minced dried shrimps, shaped into little cakes, fried then simmered with stir-fried dried mushrooms and Smithfield ham in soy and sherry.

Yu kow Fish fillets dipped in batter, deep-fried then combined with stir-fried celery cabbage, bamboo shoots and water chestnuts, served in lightly thickened sauce.

Yu riong ro bing Red snapper stuffed with minced pork and seasonings, fried then simmered in broth flavoured with ginger, brown sugar and soy.

Yu siang niu ro si Steak strips stir-fried with asparagus, covered with sauce of soy, brown beans, sherry, sugar and vinegar.

Yu shiang shiao niu ro pien Shredded marinated veal cutlets stir-fried with asparagus and covered with sauce of brown beans, sugar, soy, sherry, vinegar and ginger.

Yu siang yao hwa Pork kidneys stir-fried with bamboo shoots and mushrooms in brown bean, sherry, sugar, soy, garlic sauce.

Yu tao op Duck stuffed with taro roots, boiled in broth with ham, ginger, sherry, dried mushrooms and extra taro.

Yu tow mun wong hien Eels and taro braised with sherry, ginger, black beans and minced ham in chicken broth.

Yu tow sun kwai Eel and taro braised in chicken broth with ginger and hot pepper.

Yu yeung fooh gwaah Bitter melon disks filled with minced fish, fried then simmered in sauce of black beans and garlic.

Yu yuen Fish balls of flounder fillet, water chestnuts and scallions simmered in broth and served with duck sauce.

Yu yuen fo twei tong Fish balls simmered in chicken broth with mushrooms, bamboo shoots and celery cabbage, garnished with ham.

Yuen taai Boned ham covered with sauce of garlic, scallion, sherry, sugar and soy, fried then simmered until extremely tender, served on a bed of spinach or celery cabbage.

Yuh chi tong; yu chi tang Shark's fin soup—a banquet soup of chicken meat, beaten egg white, crab meat, shredded ham, abalone and prepared shark's fin which lends a sticky, soothing texture to the soup.

Yuh ngaum yeuhng Fish stuffed with ground lamb and wrapped in seasoning of ginger, anise, onion and vinegar, steamed.

Yuih pin tong Sliced fish in chicken broth with ginger.

Yuhn siu gwat ji gang; yuan xiao ju zi geng Glutinous rice balls filled with sugar, sesame seeds and pork fat, dropped into water and then into sweetened tangerine juice.

Yum yeung ghuy Chicken cubes covered with slices of ham and grilled.

Yung twei hwa tsai Cauliflower in ham and ginger sauce.

Yuxiang jisi Shredded chicken breast stir-fried with green pepper, red pepper and celery, flavoured with soy, sugar, chili.

Ywing er ro sih tsao don Pork strips stir-fried with cloud ears and seasonings with addition of eggs scrambled until set.

Zadin chao xianyou Stir-fried squid with carrots, broccoli, wood ears and onions in light sauce of sherry and ginger.

Zha ge li Chopped clam meat mixed with minced pork, ginger, egg and soy stuffed in clam shells and deep-fried or steamed in chicken broth.

Zha jiang mian Boiled noodles topped with minced meat sauce served with a selection of shredded vegetables to be added by the diner.

Zha ji kuai Marinated chicken pieces, floured and deep-fried.

Zha jitui Marinated chicken legs, deep-fried.

Zha niu li ji Marinated fillet of beef, coated with batter and deep-fried, served with sesame oil and spiced salt.

Zha xie Chopped crab coated in batter and deep-fried.

Zheng dan Simple steamed eggs topped with scallions.

Zheng jidan Eggs topped with chopped ham, spinach and prawns, steamed.

Zheng long xia Lobster halves topped with condiments and steamed, served with dips.

Zinhua yushu ji Boned chicken delicately simmered, sliced and arranged in alternating layers with ham served surrounded by a ring of braised broccoli or spinach leaves.

Useful words

The purpose of this section is to enable the diner to become acquainted with the most common methods of Chinese cookery and the most commonly used ingredients so that the diner may be able to piece together the ingredients of a dish listed on a menu but not in this guide; and also to gain a picture of the manner in which it is cooked.

Wherever possible, they are listed in Cantonese and Mandarin transliterations although, as was stated in the introduction, there is no one accepted transliterated form of the Chinese language.

Ba gok; ba chio Star anise – a pungent, liquorice-flavoured spice.

Ba tsi; tai tsu Rice vinegar – spicy, tangy, tart.

Ban A method of cooking or presentation in which cooked and uncooked foods are combined for texture contrast.

Bao Quick-frying method of cooking in which individual flavours are retained but blended into the whole.

Bao yu Abalone – a bland, delicately flavoured mollusk.

Bing tong; bing tang Rock sugar.

Bok go; bai go Gingko nut–soft, fleshy, delicate, used in stuffing.

Bok hop; bai ho One-hundred-unities – spice from lily plant, very subtle in flavour.

Bok tsoi; bai tsai White Chinese cabbage, subtle, bland, usually crisp-cooked.

Chao Stir-frying in small amount of oil over high heat.

Ching Steaming method of cooking.

Chwin guen pei; chwin gwen pi Egg roll skins or wrappers filled with meat or fish and vegetable mixture, deep-fried.

Chu Boiling method of cooking.

Dan Egg.

Dow fu Bean cake from soy beans – bland, delicate in flavour – used as main ingredient or blended with vegetables, meat or seafood.

Dow gok; do jiao Long green Chinese beans.

Dow sa; do sa Sweet bean filling used as stuffing for pastry.

Dow si; do shih Salted, fermented black beans used as a spice for salty, tangy flavour.

Dun Slow-cooking in a closed receptacle either by steaming or in a pan of gently boiling water.

Dung gu Dried Chinese mushrooms – delicate, meaty, gelatinous texture – can be added to almost any entrée.

Dung gwa Winter melon – bland, delicate – used as a soup ingredient or candied.

Dung yong tsoi; dung yang tsai Agar agar – vegetable gum from seaweed used in salads or mixed with vegetables or meat.

Dy to soi; ta to tsai Salted turnips – salty, spicy – used as a flavouring agent or as main ingredient.

Fa gu; hwa gu Dried Chinese (flower) mushrooms.

Fa jiu; hwa jiao Anise pepper – more pungent than black pepper.

Feng Wind-drying or wind curing of food, originally utilised for preserving food but now used for the pungent flavour which this method of preservation lends to food.

Fu gwa; ku gwa Bitter melon – an extremely bitter, pungent vegetable used as a main ingredient or added to meat dishes.

Fun see; fun si Noodles of mung beans also known as bean thread.

Gai lan tsoi; chia lan tsai Chinese broccoli – similar to American broccoli but more delicate in flavour.

Gai lat; gai mo Dry mustard – a sharp, pungent seasoning.

Gai tsoi; gai tsai Mustard greens – a tangy, bitter, slightly sour vegetable used in soups and stir-fry dishes.

Ghuy ji Chicken.

Giong; jiang Fresh ginger.

Gna tsoi; lo do ya Bean sprouts from mung beans.

Gnapp; ya Duck.

Gon hahm yu; hsien yu Salted, cured fish – pungent, very fishy, blended with meat as a flavouring agent.

Gong yu chu; gan bei Dried scallops – used as a flavouring agent.

Gow tsoi; chiu tsai Chinese chives.

Gum tsum; jing tsen Lily flowers also known as golden needles, lily buds, dried tiger lilies – sweet, unusual, distinctive flavour used as garnish or mixed with other ingredients.

Ha bang; hsia bing Shrimp chips or slices – shellfish mixed in flour dough and fried.

Ha my; sha mi Dried shrimp – fishy, meaty – used as a flavouring agent, main ingredient or in stuffing.

Hahm don; hsien dan Salted or preserved duck egg – delicate, salty flavour used as main ingredient or mixed raw with meat and cooked.

Hahm ha; shien sha Shrimp paste – strong fishy, salty taste used as a flavouring agent.

Hai sum; hai sun Sea slug – fleshy, gelatinous – takes on flavour of cooking ingredients.

Ham lam; hsien lan Cured olive with salty, sweet, anise-like flavour used as a flavouring agent.

Hong Method of grilling whereby food is placed inside a big stove or closed brazier.

Hong yong bang; hsin ren bing Almond cookies.

Hosee; hao shih Chinese dried oysters – delicate, fish used as a flavouring agent.

Hoyow; hao yo Oyster sauce – condiment with delicate, meaty flavour.

Hoy jit pei; hai jih pi Jellyfish.

Hoy sin jiong; hai hsien jiang Hoisin sauce – red seasoning sauce with pungent, sweet, garlicky flavour.

Hui Process of cooking whereby a large variety of cooked and uncooked foods are put into the same stock pot to produce a semi-soup dish.

Hung jo; hung tzao Red, dried dates used as a flavouring agent.

Hung shu Red-cooking – meat or poultry is cooked slowly in a large amount of water and soy sauce to produce a rich, tasty, reddish-brown gravy and tender meat.

Jee ma yow; tze ma yu Sesame oil – strong, pungent, appetising flavour.

Jee tsoi; tze tsai Seaweed—a sea vegetable with strong, iodine-like flavour and gelatinous, tender texture.

Jian Shallow-frying method of cooking whereby food is cooked rapidly over high heat.

Jiem Poaching method of cooking.

Jin Method of cooking such that the food is not over-cooked; requires that the freshest of produce be used—usually meat or poultry is immersed in boiling water, heat is turned off and the meat or poultry is left to cook in the receding heat.

Jing yow; jiang yu Heavy soy sauce.

Jook sun; chu sun Bamboo shoots—delicate, bland vegetable with crunchy, firm texture—indispensable in Chinese cooking.

Ju Pig.

Ju yow; tsu yo Chinese bead molasses with syrupy, bittersweet flavour used as a colouring agent.

La-ee tzee; li tze Litchi fruit—bland, sweet—used as a flavouring agent, dessert or garnish for sweet-sour dishes.

Leen gnow; lien ngo Lotus root—a vegetable root with sweet, bland, delicate flavour used as an ingredient in meat or vegetarian dishes or as a garnish in soup or as a crystallised sweet.

Leen tszee; lien tze Lotus seed used as candy or flavouring agent.

Lin Method of cooking whereby hot oil is ladled over food until it is cooked.

Liu Method of cooking whereby thin slices of food are poached quickly in deep-fat.

Lo mien Egg noodles.

Lo tsow; lao tsou Dark soy sauce, an indispensable flavouring agent.

Loong gnahn; lung yen Longans—fruit with a delicate, fragrant, refreshing, distinctive taste used as a dessert, garnish or in sweet-sour dishes.

Lop chiong; la tsang Chinese pork sausage—meaty, salty, spicy, appetising—used as a flavouring agent, main ingredient, in stuffing or mixed with other meats and vegetables.

Lot yow; la yu Hot sauce made from chilli peppers.

Lu Method of cooking whereby meats are cooked in strong herbal soy-based broth; commonly known as red-cooking or hung shu.

Ma tie; ma ti Water chestnuts—delicate, meaty, crunchy, fleshy, firm, fruit-like vegetable used as a garnish, main ingredient in meat and vegetable dishes.

Mein gon: mein jing Vegetable steak—meat substitute made from wheat gluten.

Men Method of cooking whereby meat or poultry is cooked slowly over low heat.

Mien see jiong; do bahn jiang Brown or yellow bean sauce—pungent, rich sauce indispensable as a flavouring agent.

Mong yow; wang yo Caul fat—thin covering of pig's lower intestine used as a wrapping for foods to be fried or steamed.

My fun; ki fun Rice sticks—opaque, white vermicelli.

Nam yu; nan yu Red bean curd cheese fermented, with pungent flavour.

Ng hiong fun; wu hsiang Five spices powder of star anise, Chinese cinnamon, fennel, Chinese pepper and cloves—spicy, tangy flavouring agent.

Ngai gwa; chieh tze Chinese aubergine—delicate, tender, used as main ingredient or in stir-fried dishes.

Ning mung jiong Lemon sauce – spicy, tangy flavouring agent.

Niu Beef.

Noh my; noh mi Glutinous rice used for moist, slippery, thick texture.

Op gon; ya gan Cured duck liver or gizzard – strong, meaty taste used as a flavouring agent.

Pei don; pi dan Hundred-year-old eggs – duck eggs artificially aged with coating of lime, salt, ashes and tea leaves, then cured for 100 days; pungent, cheesy flavour eaten as is, boiled or steamed or used as a flavouring agent.

Shao Stewing method of cooking usually of large pieces of meat in flavoured broth.

Sheo tsoi; tientsin bai Chinese celery cabbage – bland, delicate flavour with a firm, crunchy texture used in stir-fried dishes.

Shieh dow; shieh do Snow peas – flat pea pod vegetable with crunchy texture.

Shiet lieh hung Red-in-snow – a vegetable similar to broccoli.

Shu Barbecuing – usually over charcoal on a spit or grill.

Tiem jook or **fu jook pei; tien chu** or **fu pi chi** Dried bean curd sheets used as main ingredient or in conjunction with meats and vegetables to lend texture interest.

Tong long; ping tang yea tze Chinese coconut strips treated as a confection or sweetmeat.

Tsa Deep-frying method of cooking.

Tsen pei; tsen pi Dried tangerine peel – sweet, fragrant flavouring agent.

Tsiang Foods long-seasoned in soy or bean paste.

Tso gu; tsao gu Dried grass mushrooms valued for pungent taste.

Tsu Pork.

Win yee; rin erh Cloud ears also called wood ears or silver ears; a fungus which has a subtle flavour with a gelatinous, slippery texture.

Wong dow gna; huang do ya Bean sprouts (large variety) from mung beans.

Wu dow; wu do Black beans.

Yan Foods long-seasoned in salt, not only for the purpose of preservation but mostly for the distinctive flavour such a process lends to the food – especially fish.

Ye Smoking with materials such as camphor, wood, tea leaves, sugar, to lend different flavours to the food – usually employed as one step in a multi-phase cooking process.

Yee fu mien; ee fu mien Fried egg noodles with seasoning.

Yin waw; yen wuo Protein from cliff dwelling swallow's nests – considered a great luxury by Chinese for its subtle flavour – also considered a health tonic.

Yin yoke; hsien ro Chinese bacon.

Yow yu Dried cuttlefish – salty, fishy flavour used in soup or stir-fried with vegetables.

Yu chi; yu tze Shark's fin – a great delicacy considered a 'must' in formal dinners; white, delicate flavour with soft, fragile, crunchy texture used in soups, red-cooked meats and poultry.

Yu tau Taro root – a potato-like vegetable.

Yu toe Fish tripe – fish stomach dried into sheets used for chewy, moist texture in stir-fried dishes.

Zheng Open-steaming method of cooking.

Zhu Method of cooking in water.

Zui Food soaked or marinated in wine or spirit as one step in the cooking process.

INDIA

Aab ghosh Lamb boiled in coconut milk Moslem-style.
Aam Mango, a common fruit of India.
Aam ka ras Spiced pomegranate juice.
Achar tandal Pickled cauliflower stalks.
Ahtoo curry Madras-style mutton curry in which meat is cooked with onion and curry flavouring until fairly free of moisture.
Ahtoo molee Stewed mutton or beef simmered in coconut milk flavoured with spices, ginger and chillis.
Alebele Pancakes with coconut filling.
Aliathrum Sweet fritters made with rice flour and eggs.
Aloo gobi Potatoes and cauliflower with chilli, garlic, onion and curry spices.
Alu chat Boiled potato slices mixed with chillis, tamarind and fresh coriander.
Alu mataro Peas and potatoes cooked with tomatoes, chillis and onions.
Alu parotha Potato-filled pancakes.
Amphulia Baked mango and rice.
Andi ki kari Egg curry.
Anna-nas (balls) Minced pineapples mixed with flour batter and deep-fried.
Appum Thin pancake-like hoppers of rice flour and coconut milk.
Aru Peach.
Atta roti Thin, small biscuits of wholewheat and white flour.
Avakkai mangai Mango chutney.

Badam farfi Almond fudge.
Baffat Pork or beef curry with radishes.
Baigan tamatar Aubergines and tomatoes flavoured with spices, garlic and tomato puree.
Bajre ki roti Bread made of millet flour.
Bakarknani Crisp thin bread.
Balashai Balls of flour, ground almonds and dried milk with cardamom seeds, fried to a deep brown.
Ballachong balchao Very hot pickled prawns.
Balushahi Sugar-coated doughnut-shaped breads, deep-fried.
Bangan phulouri Aubergine or onion fritter.
Barfi Milk sweetmeat decorated with almonds.
Barra kabab massamman Meat marinated in minced onion and spices, skewered and cooked over open fire grill.
Beebeek Coconut cake.
Behndi foogath Lady's fingers (okra) cooked and flavoured with chillis, onion, garlic and green ginger.
Bengal dhall Boiled lentils flavoured with thick paste of curry spices and minced garlic and onion.
Besani roti Fried bread made of chick peas (garbanzo beans) and melted butter (ghee).
Beveca A baked pudding of rice flour, coconut milk and sugar.

Bhaji Vegetables cooked to absorb heat of chillis and spices —very hot and dry; the word can also refer to deep-fried fritters.

Bhaji (potato) Potatoes fried with onion, garlic, mustard seed and spices.

Bhaji (spinach) Spinach stir-fried with onion, garlic and spices.

Bhang A liquid preparation made of leaves and flowers of marijuana plant mixed with milk, chopped almonds, ginger, drunk on special religious holidays.

Bhat aur savia An Anglo-Indian dish of rice and spaghetti flavoured with onion, garlic, cloves and cinnamon.

Bhatura Deep-fried leavened bread of flour and chick peas eaten as a snack food in the Punjab area.

Bhelpuri Small, deep-fried breads served with chopped onion, puffed rice, boiled potatoes, lemon juice and chutney.

Bhindi bhaji Lady's fingers (okra) fried in a mixture of onion, garlic and spices.

Bhoona ghosht Dry curries common to southern India in which spiced lamb or beef is fried in spices until meat absorbs most of the cooking liquid.

Bhugias Deep-fried dough flavoured with chillis, curry spices and usually mixed with a combination of vegetables.

Bhujiya Potatoes and aubergine cooked with pepper, chilli, ginger and mustard.

Biryani Rice cooked with curry sauce and meat garnished with pepper, hard-boiled eggs and tomatoes.

Biryani (vegetable) Elaborate rice dish of mixed vegetables such as carrots, peas, cauliflower, aubergine flavoured with spices, chillis, garlic and ginger.

Bommaloe machee (Bombay Duck) A small fish of the Bombay region salted and dried in the sun until stiff, fried and served as a snack, side dish or used as a flavouring agent in a curry.

Boorthas Moslem-style savoury dishes served with pillaus, kitcherees (rice and lentils) and coconut rice.

Boti kabab Meat cubes marinated, skewered and cooked over open fire.

Brinjal boortha Pulped boiled aubergines mixed with minced onion, chillis, coconut milk, olive oil and lemon juice.

Brinjal ka tikka Baked aubergine with vegetable stuffing.

Brinjal mussala cutlets Aubergine shells filled with flavoured aubergine pulp, coated in breadcrumbs and eggs and fried.

Budhuk aur mutter Duck and green pea curry.

Budhuk ka korma Duck pieces marinated in dhye (sour curds) simmered in a mixture of minced onion, cloves, garlic, cardamoms and cinnamon; a rich and spicy dish but not peppery hot, usually served with pillau, kitcheree (rice cooked with lentils) or coconut rice.

Budhuk ka salun Decca-style duck curry flavoured with thick coconut milk and lemon juice.

Cacjiubar A general name for salads but specifically refers to an onion salad spiced with hot chillis.

Calcutta kari Beef curry of which there are many variations but most well-known are probably the beef curries of Madras and Calcutta—beef cubes are pre-simmered and then recooked with curry spices, garlic, onion, ghee, coconut milk and chillis (the amount depending upon taste).

Chaat Fruit salad of bananas, oranges, pears, apples, guavas, spiced with chilli powder, ginger and lemon juice.

Chai Tea – usually drunk with milk and honey or sugar.

Chana dal Split chick peas cooked with chillis, turmeric, cumin, coriander, tamarind pulp, mustard seeds and garlic.

Chana dal khichadi Brown or white rice cooked with split chick peas flavoured with butter, garlic and chillis.

Chapati Wholewheat unleavened griddle bread.

Chawal Plain boiled rice.

Chawal roti narul Bread of rice flour and desiccated coconut.

Chawal soogee poorees Wheat and rice flour balls with cardamom seeds formed into small biscuits, deep-fried and soaked in rose-flavoured syrup.

Chikkis Fried balls of flour, sugar, butter and sesame seeds eaten as a snack food or with tea.

Chingri jhoal Spicy shrimp curry with flaked coconut.

Chirga Whole chicken rubbed with cayenne, paprika, lime juice, vinegar, then coated with a paste of yoghurt, green ginger, onion, salt and pepper, roasted on an open spit.

Chirupayaru payasam Sweet lentils served during Onam festival.

Chitchkee Vegetable curry of peas, carrots, turnips, tomatoes, potatoes, runners and other vegetables in season.

Chivra A snack food of split chick peas, chopped nuts, puffed rice and raisins flavoured with spices, lemon and sugar.

Chuckolee Delicate pastry of flour and butter cut into diamond shapes and simmered in cinnamon and sugar milk.

Chundole Cooked meat simmered with onion, garlic, chillis and ginger – a dry curry of Mogul origin.

Chutney An essential condiment of India used as an added flavour and as an appetite stimulator, usually very hot and spicy, served in small quantities. Two types of chutney predominate – fresh and preserved, and can be made of almost any vegetable or fruit but are always heavily spiced: **kothmir** coriander chutney; **mooroongakai** drumstick chutney; **poothena** mint chutney; **pullee** or **imli** tamarind chutney; **purpoo** dhall chutney; **thainga** coconut chutney; **thucahley** green tomato chutney.

Chourisam Spicy pork and liver sausage from Goa.

Copra kana Rice cooked in coconut milk, either plain or spicy, sometimes coloured with turmeric.

Dahi Curd or yoghurt.

Dhall Literally means split lentil but now refers to the soup-like preparation made from it. No Indian meal is complete without this dish, the simplest meal usually consisting of rice and dhall: **dhall aur bhagi** lentils with spinach flavoured with onions and pickled chillis; **dhall bath** rice served with lentils; **dhall bghari** lentils with onions or garlic, eaten as a side dish; **dhall cha** meat cooked in spices, chillis, ginger and onion then simmered with prepared lentils; **dhall curry** boiled lentils simmered in curry sauce, garlic, onion, chillis and tomato paste; **dhall dahi** Mogul-style lentil curry flavoured with cinnamon and cloves; **dhall dahi bara** lentil cakes in yoghurt; **dhall dahi vada** deep-fried dough of ground lentils flavoured with chilli, spices and yoghurt; **dhall degh bhurta mhaans** meat, usually lamb, with chick peas, lentils and dumplings that have been poached in yoghurt; **dhall dokia** batter of lentil, rice and chillis steamed then fried; **dhall dhokali** lentil soup flavoured with chillis, spices, lemon juice, tomato and mustard seed with dumplings made of chick pea flour; **dhall dosas** savoury pancakes of ground lentil and rice flour flavoured with chillis sometimes filled with potatoes or other vegetables; **dhall dur byngun** lentils and aubergines flavoured with chillis, garlic and onion; **dhall rissoles** lentils mixed with minced onion and garlic until the consistency of porridge then blended with chillis, egg and flour formed into balls and deep-fried; **dhall shoorva** lentils cooked with onion and passed through a sieve then flavoured with chillis, garlic, green ginger, butter and sour curds; **tarka dhall** spiced lentil puree.

Diliya dosa Oat pancakes.

Doodhi-chana-nu-shak Split chick peas and doodhi (a gourd vegetable much like zucchini) flavoured with ginger, garlic, mustard seeds and curry spices.

Dopiazah Lamb cubes stir-fried with onions, spices and chillis then simmered until tender with addition of more onions to give texture contrast to cooked onions.

Ekoori Scrambled eggs with tomatoes, onions, chillis and spices.

Firni Cream of rice pudding with almonds and pistachios flavoured with rosewater and butter.

Foogaths Savoury dishes made with cooked vegetables— almost any vegetable can be used but freshly scraped coconut is usually an essential ingredient in a proper foogath: **behndi** foogath of lady's fingers (okra); **gager ka** foogath of carrots; **govee ka** foogath of cabbage; **kayla ka** foogath of bananas; **mochokotay** foogath of haricot, butter or broad beans; **mooroongkai** drumstick foogath flavoured with garlic, chillis and curry spices; **thucahley** foogath of tomatoes.

Gajar kanji Cold carrot drink with mustard seed and chilli.

Gajar kheer Rich, sweet carrot pudding with raisins and slivered almonds.

Garam masala A powder of ground cardamoms, coriander seeds, cumin, cloves and peppercorns which forms the base of much Indian cookery.

Ghee Clarified butter widely used in Indian cooking.

Ghiya bhajia A snack food of little balls made of grated ghiya (a cucumber-like vegetable), chick pea flour, spices and chilli, deep-fried, served with yoghurt.

Ghiya-ka-kofta Little balls of grated ghiya and chick pea flour flavoured with cayenne deep-fried and served in a sauce of onion and tomatoes flavoured with ginger, chilli and curry spices.

Ghiya-ka-shak Ghiya stir-fried with mustard seed, garlic, tamarind pulp, chillis and curry spices.

Ghobi aur matar Cauliflower and peas flavoured with mustard seeds, cayenne and lemon juice.

Ghosht aur aloo Meat and potato curry.

Ghosht do pyaza Meat cooked with onions.

Ghosht ka korma Lamb or mutton pieces cooked in Mogul-style with onions, garlic, ginger, dhye (sour curds), ground almonds and flaked coconut.

Ghosht ka salun Pieces of lean beef simmered to tenderness and blended in a paste of spices, ginger, chillis and coconut milk.

Ghosht ka shoorva Mutton soup (mulligatawny) seasoned with chillis, garlic, thick coconut milk and lemon juice.

Ghota ka ghagi Cooked spinach condimented with onion, garlic, chillis and oil.

Goanese stick kabab Mutton and pork cubes skewered alternately with green ginger slices cooked in a mixture of onion, garlic, chillis until a thick gravy forms.

Gobi mhaans Braised meat with cauliflower.

Golgappa Deep-fried wafers served with potatoes and sweet-sour sauce.

Goolab jamon Little rolls of dried milk and ground almonds deep-fried and coated with heavy sugar syrup.

Gudumba Mango drink with cumin and cardamom flavouring.

Halva (banana) Mashed bananas fried with sugar, flavoured with spices and almonds.

Halva (carrot) Grated carrots cooked in milk until thick mixed with chopped almonds, honey and butter.

Halva (date) Ground dates mixed with ground almonds, honey and cardamom seeds and fried in ghee (clarified butter).

Hazur pasand Rice with meat, fruit and nuts.

Hoppers Crisp rice pancakes.

Hurran ka gosht kabab Venison steaks rubbed with a paste of lemon juice, turmeric, ground chillis then grilled or fried.

Jalle bi Pretzel-like sweets coated with syrup.

Jhal fry Any cold meat stir-fried in curry spices, onion, garlic, chilli, ginger, tamarind pulp.

Jhinga kari Madrasi Madras-style dry shrimp curry—shrimps stir-fried until coated with curry spices.

Jhinga sambal Cooked shrimps and hard-boiled eggs served in sauce of coconut milk, onion, garlic, chilli, lemon juice garnished with peas and coriander leaves.

Jhinga pathia Shrimps simmered in coconut milk flavoured with garlic, ginger, spices, tomato puree.

Jungli budhuk ka salun Wild duck gently simmered in curry sauce and coconut milk.

Kababs Large pieces of meat cooked in their own juices or smaller pieces skewered and grilled over open fire or minced and formed into cutlets and fried: **hoosaini** minced beef or mutton mixed with spices, garlic and onion blended with egg, shaped into oval cutlets and fried; **kooftah** minced mutton or beef balls mixed with chopped onion, garlic and sour curds, cooked slowly until the meat is tender and has absorbed the marinade; **moglai hoosaini** minced mutton cooked in spices, desiccated coconut and almonds; **sami** minced mutton mixed with spices, chillis and coconut flakes, formed into oval cutlets and fried; **seekh** mutton pieces marinated, skewered with tiny onions and slices of green ginger then roasted over a grill; **shikampooree** minced meat cooked in spices and coconut milk; **tikkah machchi** marinated fish skewered and grilled.

Kachoris Pastry balls stuffed with a spicy lentil or potato filling.

Kadhi Yoghurt curry or a hot and spicy soup with curry spices.

Kadoo Pumpkin.

Kakadi Cucumber.

Kala chana Small black chick pea.

Kala chana aur alu A sharp and spicy dish of chick peas and potatoes.

Kaleja sheesh Spiced liver with onions.

Kayla (balls) Banana pulp batter, deep-fried.

Keftas Savoury meatballs stuffed with a mixture of chillis, garlic, ginger and onions with cinnamon stick and cardamom then simmered in tomato sauce.

Kekra Crab.

Kesar doodh Saffron milk flavoured with cloves, cinnamon, chopped almonds and honey.

Kesar pillau A sweet dish traditionally served on special feast days – rice cooked in ghee with raisins, pistachio nuts, almonds, spices and sugar.

Kesari-bhat Saffron rice flavoured with sliced almonds, raisins, butter.

Kesari chawal Saffron rice.

Khagina Spiced omelette.

Khata mung Mung beans with yoghurt and garlic chutney.

Kheema (beef) Minced beef fried with onions, garlic, grated ginger, spices and chillis.

Kheem aur bhagi Minced meat and lettuce curry.

Kheema aur mattar Minced meat with peas.

Kheer Cream of rice pudding flavoured with cardamom, honey, raisins and rosewater.

Khichadi Rice and lentils flavoured with turmeric and butter.

Kholee molee Chicken cooked in coconut milk and spices.

Khubab hans Roast goose.

Khumbi Mushrooms.

Kitcheree Rice and lentils cooked with garlic, ginger, spices, onions and butter, served garnished with hard-boiled eggs and crisp fried onions.

Kooftah Balls of minced mutton or beef, blended with onions, garlic, ginger and spices and cooked in a curry sauce which is made to taste and varies according to the locality – prawns and fish can also be used for this dish.

Kooftah kari Meatballs deep-fried and blended in a curry sauce.

Kooftah pillau Minced mutton or beef blended with garlic, spices formed into balls and cooked in rice pillau (rice cooked with seasonings).

Kooftah shami machchi Fish croquettes.

Kool Boiled flour balls broken down into a gruel with sour milk.

Korma A dish braised with yoghurt and/or cream – usually rich and spicy though rarely very hot; **badam malai khatai** lamb korma with cream and almonds; **bahadhar shahi** braised lamb in a mild but rich korma dish of almonds, yoghurt, double cream and egg yolks; **budduck ka** duck korma; **dil-pasand** braised meat and vegetables in a mellow garlic sauce; **ghosht ka** lamb or mutton korma; **hazur pasand** a special braised lamb dish finished with egg white and a mixture of nuts, raisins and saffron; **jogurath** meat braised in spices and yoghurt and finished with double cream; **kasa** casserole of meatballs with vegetables; **morgee** chicken korma; **roghan josh** lamb korma; **sadah** plain meat korma in yoghurt.

Koykotay Steamed balls of rice flour, brown sugar and coconut milk batter.

Kulee Boiled flour balls served with hot vegetable curries.

Kurghosh ka salun Rabbit slowly simmered in curry sauce until tender and the gravy is thick and rich.

Kurlieachi kari Crab curry.

Madoo curry Madras beef curry with tomato paste.

Madras buffath Thick cut slices of beef simmered with potatoes, carrots, spring onions in sauce of onions, garlic, ginger, curry spices, chillis and cooked until most of the liquid is absorbed by the meat and vegetables.

Madras fried fish Fish fillets marinated in paste of turmeric, chillis, onions, garlic and lemon juice, fried.

Madras hulwa A sweet of desiccated coconut, cardamoms, poppy seeds, sugar and ghee.

Matar panir Curry of peas (or other vegetable) and Indian cheese in a light sauce with tomatoes.

Meeta anna-nas puthole Sweet pineapple puffs.

Meeta dhall pustholes Sweet puffs of lentils, coconut flakes, cardamoms, cloves and cinnamon sweetened to taste.

Meeta kayla pustholes Sweet banana puffs.

Meeta naral pusthole Sweet coconut puffs with raisins and ground almonds.

Moglai chicken Whole chicken marinated in sour curd sauce, roasted or baked.

Moglai chops Lamb or mutton chops marinated in sour curds, spices, chillis, ginger and garlic and sautéed with ghee.

Molee Essentially a dish of vegetables, eggs, fish or other seafoods based on a sauce of coconut milk, onions, garlic, chillis, ginger, turmeric, ghee or butter: **khoiee** cold cooked chicken pieces simmered in molee sauce; **kutherakoi** fried aubergines simmered in molee; **madoo** beef or mutton slowly stewed in molee; **meen** fish simmered in molee sauce; **mootay** eggs hardboiled and served with molee sauce poured over them; **vathoo** cold roast duck boned and skinned, warmed in molee.

Moorgee cutlets Minced cooked chicken meat mixed with minced onions, chillis, ginger, spices, mint, formed into cutlets, fried.

Mooroongakai curry Curry of drumstick vegetables and mutton cubes fried in ghee with onion and garlic and simmered in coconut milk and finally finished with lemon juice and thick coconut milk.

Muchlee curry Eels in curry sauce with garlic, onion, tomatoes.

Muchlee imlee Salt fish washed in vinegar and dried, then packed in a pickle sauce of corianders, turmeric, chillis, ginger and garlic, allowed to age; when ready, it is fried in ghee or butter.

Mulligatawny A soup of the British colonials, literally translated as 'pepper water', usually made of beef stock, ghee, onion, spices, chillis, tamarind water but there are many variations of this soup – with chicken stock, mutton, beef, vegetables, dhall (lentils) - rice, curry sauce.

Mussala beef steak Meat rubbed with paste of corianders, cumin seed, mustard seed, turmeric and chillis, fried in ghee.

Mutchakotay Haricot or butter beans curry.

Naan Baked leavened bread.

Nareal Coconut.

Nareal ka chawal Coconut-flavoured rice.

Navrattan sabzi dum Steamed mixed vegetables.

Nimbu ka chawal Lime-flavoured rice.

Nimbu pani Sweetened fresh lime juice.

Ola Baked and mashed aubergines fried with yoghurt and spices.

Oothappam Spicy pancake of rice flour and ground lentils.

Pachadi Vegetables such as potatoes, onions, cauliflowers or okra cooked with curd and chillis usually served cold.

Pakki hui machli Baked fish with coriander and spices.

Pakoras Spiced fritters of chick peas sometimes served on its own but often used as a coating for fresh vegetables, particularly spinach.

Palak paneer Spinach and cheese dish.

Palak shalgam Spinach and turnip dish.

Pancha dhall A holiday dish of five varieties of lentils cooked with spices flavoured with lemon juice and served with flaked fresh coconut.

Panir A simple curd cheese eaten alone but also used in vegetable curries.

Panyarum Batter of rice flour, mashed bananas and brown sugar fried in deep-fat.

Papad Thin, brittle potato-chip like pieces of fried dough eaten as a side item.

Paratha Wholewheat griddle-fried bread made with ghee or butter sometimes stuffed with spiced meat or vegetables.

Parcha kabab yakhni Rolled mutton with spices and eggs.

Parcha seekhi Leg of lamb rubbed with flavourings and cooked on a spit.

Parotha Chapatis rolled together to make a multi-layered bread roasted with ghee spread.

Pasanda Beef slices marinated in yoghurt, fried in ghee and simmered until tender with garlic, onion and curry spices.

Patiyas Potatoes cooked with green bananas.

Patrani matchli Pomfret (a common fish of India) stuffed with green chutney, wrapped in banana leaves and steamed.

Payasam Semi-liquid sweet rice dessert.

Peras Sweetmeat made of khoy and pistachios flavoured with cardamom or nutmeg.

Petha Sweetmeat made of white pumpkin.

Philouries Deep-fried pieces of lentil flour dough flavoured with chillis and curry spices.

Phoolkay A small puffed-up chapati cooked on a griddle.

Phul varbia Small, dried rice puffs.

Phulgobi bharta Cauliflower puree.

Pillau A combination of rice and meats or vegetables cooked in ghee or butter and then slowly simmered in saffron and spices-flavoured water.

Pootoo rice Glutinous, rich rice used for sweet dishes of which there are two types: the white variety is steamed and served with coconut and granulated sugar; the black is ground into flour and is used for making a sweetmeat called **tho-thole** rich with ghee, almonds and fruit.

Pootoo rice balls Balls made of rice flour filled with coconut and sugar, boiled and rolled in freshly grated coconut.

Pootoo rice fritters Fritters of mashed banana pulp, rice flour, eggs, coconut milk and sugar.

Pudda Salted fish pickled in vinegar and tamarind water, macerated and blended with a paste of chillis, ginger and spices and left to age; when ready for use, it is formed into cakes and is fried in ghee or butter.

Pudla A pancake-like omelette with chick pea flour dough, spices, tomatoes, onions, ginger and chillis.

Puli ingi Hot ginger curry.

Punny kari Pork cubes fried with onion, garlic, ginger, chillis simmered in curry spices.

Punjabi chana Chick peas cooked with spices and eaten with rice or as a snack with yoghurt.

Puran poli Bread stuffed with sweet lentil filling flavoured with cardamom seeds.

Puri Deep-fried wholewheat bread, a traditional breakfast food eaten with chutney.

Pusindah seekhi Marinated lamb cubes skewered and grilled.

Pustholes Fried pieces of dough with chutney filling.

Pyazwale khare masale ka gosht Meat with spices and onions.

Pyazwale sookhe aloo Fried mashed potatoes and onions flavoured with spices, peppers and lemon juice.

Raan ka kabab Marinated leg of lamb cooked in its spicy yoghurt marinade.

Raeta Vegetable salad combined with yoghurt to make a refreshing salad – the most common being a combination of cucumber, tomatoes and onion in unflavoured yoghurt garnished with coriander.

Rarrah Saddle of lamb.

Ras malai Cream cheese balls in cream or thickened milk.

Rasgollah Little balls of milk curds served in rose-flavoured syrup.

Rogha josh Lamb pieces marinated in yoghurt, ginger, chillis, cooked with spices in marinade until tender.

Roghni nan Flat leavened bread baked in oven.

Rogna roti Saffron-flavoured and coloured cakes of wheat flour and semolina baked on a griddle.

Sabat maahn Small black lentils cooked with spices and chillis until mushy, then fried in ghee with onions; an essential dish at a wedding feast of the Punjab area.

Sabzi mughiai Mixed vegetables with almonds, pistachio nuts and spices cooked in ghee and yoghurt.

Sabzi pillau Rice with mixed vegetables.

Sag mhaans Mild, garlicky meat dish with spinach and yoghurt.

Sagh Spinach but sometimes refers to green vegetables in general.

Saioo Deep-fried dough of rice flour, chillis, turmeric passed through a sieve or mould so that the flour pieces look like spaghetti.

Sambals Side dishes always served with main course of which there are countless variations depending on the ingredients available and the ingenuity of the cook. The basic dressing is of onions, garlic, chillis, curry spices and is served as a sauce of coconut milk flavoured with chopped onions, chillis and garlic: **aloo ka** potato cubed and blended with chopped chillis, onion and lemon juice; **behndi** lady's fingers (okra) with sambal sauce; **belatee bygun ka** fresh tomatoes, onions, chillis, lemon juice sprinkled with flaked coconut; **ginga aur undah ka** whole prawns and hard-boiled eggs covered with sambal sauce of thick coconut milk garnished with green peas; **ginga ka** prawns cooked and blended with a sambal dressing, thick coconut milk and flaked coconut, served cold or hot with hardboiled eggs; **kayla ka** green bananas cut into thin slices and sprinkled with ground chillis blended with sambal sauce; **kutherakai** aubergine roasted and the pulp mashed and mixed with chopped onion, chillis and coconut milk; **mochokotay** butter or haricot beans tossed in sambal mixture; **moorgee ka** shredded chicken breast tossed in freshly grated coconut and dusted with chilli flakes and served with lemon-flavoured sambal sauce; **muchlee ka** flaked fish mixed with sambal sauce, desiccated coconut and parsley; **peaz ka** sliced onions with fresh or pickled chillis and lemon juice; **sa-oo** sour apples cut into small cubes, sprinkled with ground chillis and lemon juice and blended with sambal sauce; **thainga** desiccated coconut blended with onions, chillis and sambal sauce; **tharkari ka** a macedoine containing carrots, peas, beans, turnips and potatoes served with sambal sauce; **undah ka** hardboiled eggs coated with sambal sauce.

Sambhar Aubergine, cauliflower, potato, onion and other vegetables cooked with lentils in a spicy hot sauce.

Samosa Flour dough shells filled with vegetable mixture cooked in spices, ginger and onion, deep-fried.

Saunf Aniseed eaten as a digestive after meals.

Serpathala Spicy dish made with pigs' blood, liver and pork.

Sesame chikkis Sesame seeds, ghee, whole wheat flour and brown sugar cooked and formed into balls eaten as a sweet snack.

Sev Noodles of chick pea flour flavoured with chilli pepper.

Sev-biranja Indian wheat noodles boiled and stir-fried in ghee with brown sugar sometimes eaten as a rice or bread substitute.

Shahjahani biriani Spiced saffron rice with lamb – spicy, festive dish often garnished with silver leaf.

Shahi pillau Rice with almonds, cream, yoghurt, light spices and butter.

Sharbat Chilled drink made from fruits, flower petals or nuts.

Shythani kabab ka salun Minced meat curry.

Sindhi gosht Lamb marinated in spicy sauce and grilled.

Soojee bhugia Fritters of onion, garlic, chillis, flour and milk, deep-fried.

Sorpotel Pickled pork casserole.

Subh degh Cubed lamb cooked with spices served with cooked and pickled vegetables and yoghurt.

Suvar mas ka salun Pork curry.

Suvar mas lorma Pork braised with yoghurt and sometimes honey.

Suvar mas vindalu Hot south Indian vinegar curry.

Tandoori The word for a charcoal-fired brick oven in which poultry and skewered meat are cooked.

Tandoori murgh Chicken pieces marinated in spices, lemon juice, ginger and onions roasted in a tandoori oven, garnished with lettuce leaves, tomatoes and onion rings.

Tandoori roti Wholewheat flat bread cooked in a tandoori oven.

Tarka dal Lentils cooked in a spicy broth mixed with tarka sauce of sesame oil, garlic, chillis and coriander seeds.

Thucahley foogaths Stewed tomatoes flavoured with chillis, spices and desiccated coconut.

Tikka kabab A popular street-corner snack of northern India; lamb cubes marinated in spices, yoghurt and lemon juice, skewered and grilled over charcoal fires.

Tho thole A pudding of black pootoo rice flour, sugar, coconut milk and sliced almonds.

Tholtee Strips of meat rubbed with a paste of vinegar, chillis and curry spices and left to dry in the sun then stored for later use.

Undah khitcherie Scrambled eggs with onions, tomatoes, chilli and coriander.

Urad dal yoghurt Split beans cooked in yoghurt broth, spices, garlic and ginger until thick and spicy, flavoured with lemon juice.

Upma Cream of wheat flavoured with spices, garlic.

Uppama Vegetables, nuts, vermicelli, fried with herbs and spices then simmered until the mixture is thick.

Vadda Small savoury fried snacks made from lentil or chick pea flour, grated vegetables, ground nuts, and spices – served dry with chutney or soaked in yoghurt.

Vadhar bhat Cooked rice fried with onion, ginger, spices, seasoned with lemon juice.

Varak Very fine, edible gold or silver leaf used to garnish elaborate dishes.

Vathoo kari Madras-style duck curry with chillis and cumin seed flavoured with lemon juice and coconut milk.

Vengi bath Aubergine and rice flavoured with spices and onion.

Vindaloos The curry of southern India – much hotter and more vinegary than the northern version, utilising rich meats such as fat pork, fat ducks and geese: **madoo** beef vindaloo; **punny** pork vindaloo; **vathoo** duck vindaloo.

Yoghurt An important food of India often served alone as a side dish, cooked with vegetables, used as a marinade base, used to make sweet-sour puddings and as a base for hot or sweet sauces.

Zarda A raisin, rice and saffron dessert.

Useful words

Chai Tea.

Chasnidarh Sweet and sour flavour of lime juice or vinegar and sugar.

Degh The word means 'pot', hence a casserole dish.

Dum A cooking technique wherein food is steamed between two fires.

Garam masala A blend of ground mixed spices – cinnamon, cloves, cardamom, cumin, coriander and black peppercorns, usually added to a dish just before serving.

Ghee Clarified butter.

Hari mirchi Green chillis.

Kafi Coffee.

Kari Sauce of spice mixture, the base of curry.

Massalam A spiced or savoury dish.

Molee South Indian white curry made of coconut milk, green chillis, ginger and spices.

Mulligatawny An Anglo-Indian spicy soup with meat stock as a base.

Paneer Curd cheese.

Parcha Meat or vegetables, rolled and often stuffed before being roasted.

Sambals Indian *hors d'oeuvre* but often served as side dishes or accompaniments to a main dish.

Seek An iron skewer, thus indicating that the food is skewered.

Sharbat Chilled drink made from fruits, flower petals or nuts.

Tandoori Food cooked in clay oven of intense heat – meat is usually marinated in yoghurt and spices previous to cooking.

Tikki Cutlet or cake.

INDONESIA

Abon Strongly flavoured dish of meat, prawns or fish meant to be eaten in small amounts with bland rice.

Abon daging Beef simmered until tender then grated and mixed with spices, fried with coconut milk and left to dry in oven until all the liquid is absorbed, used in small amounts to flavour rice.

Acar ikan Whole fish rubbed with turmeric, fried then simmered in sauce of chillis, onions, vinegar and macademia nuts.

Acar kuning Cooked vegetable mixture dressed with spices, vinegar, brown sugar and mustard.

Agar-agar dengan A pudding of agar agar (seaweed) dissolved in sugar water mixed with egg custard mixture and steamed.

Ajam bali Chicken fried in sauce of chillis, macademia nuts, ginger and coriander, Balinese-style without coconut milk.

Ajam boemboe opor Chicken pieces browned and simmered with Indonesian spices and coconut milk.

Ajam boemboe roedjak Browned chicken pieces simmered in coconut milk and spice mixture of onion, cloves, hot pepper sauce (sambal badjak), dried shrimp paste (trassu), vinegar and sugar.

Ajam bumbu rudjak Whole chicken split and flattened, simmered in hot chilli-coconut milk sauce then grilled or roasted over an open fire.

Ajam goreng padang Chicken fried in hot sauce Sumatra-style.

Ajam ketjap Chicken pieces marinated in Indonesian soy sauce (ketjap), lemon juice, garlic and oil, broiled.

Ajam kuning Chicken simmered in savoury sauce based on coconut milk but without chillis.

Ajam semur djawa Javanese-style chicken cooked in sauce of chillis, onion, garlic, soy and chopped tomato.

Apem Yeast pancakes of coconut liquid, rice flour, eggs and sugar served with melted butter and sugar.

Asinan Cucumber, onion and chilli pepper salad with sweet-sour dressing.

Atjar ketimun Cucumbers pickled in vinegar, sugar and chillis.

Atjar tjampur atau kuning Vegetables such as cauliflower, cucumber, carrots, cabbage or green beans pickled in vinegar, chillis and sugar.

Ayam bali Fried chicken simmered in sauce of nuts, green ginger, chillis, soy, sugar and vinegar.

Ayam goreng jawa Chicken pieces simmered in broth flavoured with garlic, shallots and spices, deep-fried.

Ayam panggang kecap Roasted chicken rubbed with soy and seasoning, grilled.

Babi guling Suckling pig stuffed with spice mixture and fried onions, roasted.

Babi kecap Pork slices floured and fried, served in a sweet-sour sauce with tomatoes.

Babi ketjap Pork cubes simmered in spice mixture of soy, ginger, garlic and brown sugar.

Babi taotjo Pork cubes simmered in spice mixture of soy, and brown beans served with braised scallions.

Bahmie goreng Fried noodles Chinese-style topped with chicken meat and vegetables in a sauce of chicken stock flavoured with soy, chillis and onions.

Bebek betutu Spiced duckling wrapped in banana leaves and baked in embers.

Bebek hijau Duck pieces simmered in spicy green chili sauce.

Bebotok Ground beef mixed with eggs and coconut milk flavoured with spice mixture and steamed.

Begedel djagung Sweet corn fritters.

Boemboe bali Boiled beef refried in spice mixture of sambal badjak (chilli-onion flavouring), lemon and Indonesian soy sauce.

Brengkesan Fish fillets covered in sauce of sambal badjak (chilli-onion flavouring), vinegar and nuts, broiled.

Dadar djawa Javanese omelette of eggs, onion, chillis and soy.

Dadar tahoe Omelette of bean curds and eggs flavoured with bacon, onion, ginger and soy sauce.

Daging masak bali Meat slices simmered in Balinese-style sauce of chillis, onions, garlic, ginger and brown sugar.

Dendang pedas Thin slices of meat coated in spices and dried in the sun until brittle then stir-fried with chillis and garlic.

Dendang ragi Thin slices of beef stewed with chillis, spices and desiccated coconut, fried until the liquid is absorbed and the meat slices are crispy.

Gado gado Vegetable salad with peanut and coconut milk dressing – vegetable can be a selection of cooked or fresh – whatever is in season or desired.

Gule Curry of Indian origin adapted to Indonesian cuisine.

Gule ajam Chicken pieces simmered in a curry sauce of chillis, coconut milk, lemon grass, macademia nuts and spices.

Gule djawa Curry of central Java of mutton in curry sauce without chillis, slightly sweetened.

Gule ikan padang Sumatra-style curry usually of whole fish steamed in curry sauce of chillis, spices, coconut milk, lemon grass.

Gule kambing Mutton curry of west Java in sauce of chillis, tomatoes and ground coconut; gule kambing of north Sumatra is differentiated from that of west Java in the use of fennel and cumin in the basic chilli and coconut juice sauce.

Gule masin ikan Sumatra-style curry of fish fillets.

Gule pakis Mixed vegetables in Sumatra-style curry sauce flavoured with chillis and coconut milk and spices.

Gule udang dengan labu kuning Sumatra-style curry of prawns and winter squash simmered in coconut milk, chillis, lemon grass.

Ikan asam manis Fish simmered in sweet-sour sauce of sugar, vinegar, tamarind juice and spices.

Ikan bakar Fish fillets rubbed with lime juice and garlic, grilled and served with a sauce of tomatoes, chillis and soy.

Ikan bandang panggang Boned fish rubbed with paste of ground onion, garlic and salt, baked with soy, lemon juice and chilli.

Ikan masak bali Balinese-style fish fried and simmered in broth flavoured with tamarind pulp, soy, ginger, garlic and spices.

Ikan selyr dhawa Fish cutlets soaked in tamarind water and fried, served with sauce of chillis, onions, garlic and soy.

Ikan tjuka Sumatra-style fish fried and simmered in ginger, onion, chilli and vinegar-flavoured sauce.

Kambling rendang Lamb slices stir-fried with onion, lemon peel, chilli powder, turmeric and salt, simmered with coconut milk thickened with coconut flakes.

Kelia ayam Chicken curry with chillis, shallots and spices.

Kerrie ikan Deep-fried fish fillets simmered in spice mixture of coriander, cumin, ginger, garlic, lemon grass and coconut milk.

Ketupat Boiled glutinous rice wrapped in coconut leaf.

Kormah kambing Mutton cubes marinated in spice mixture of coriander seeds, cumin, peppercorns, ginger and onion, then fried in butter with cinnamon, cloves, garlic, onion and lemon grass, finally simmered in coconut milk thickened with potatoes.

Krupuk Shrimp or prawn crackers fried until puffy served with drinks as an appetiser or with meals.

Kwee pilow Indonesian-style doughnut balls.

Kwee talam Brown and white pudding of brown sugar and white, coconut milk, rice flour.

Lapis daging semarang Meat slices marinated in paste of onion, garlic, pepper, nutmeg, sugar and soy stir-fried and simmered with tomatoes.

Lepat bugis Steamed pudding of coconut, brown sugar and rice flour.

Lontong Long grain rice boiled in plastic bags or more traditionally in banana leaves until compressed into a firm mass–served cold, sliced.

Nasi djagoeng Rice and corn cooked together.

Nasi goering Savoury rice cooked in coconut milk without spices.

Nasi goreng Indonesian-style fried rice with meat, omelette strips, cucumber slices flavoured with soy, sambal badjak (pepper-onion paste).

Nasi kebuli Chicken simmered in flavoured broth of spices, onion and garlic, fried in butter and served on a mound of rice cooked with butter, garnished with fried onion flakes and celery.

Nasi koening Long grain white rice cooked in coconut milk and turmeric flavoured with lemon grass, bay leaf, served with a garnish of cucumber slices, hardboiled eggs and fried onion flakes.

Nasi soto ajam Chicken boiled in flavoured stock, boned and shredded, served with plates of hardboiled eggs, vegetables, potato crisps and fried vermicelli with chicken broth ladled over all, eaten with rice and sambal.

Oblok-oblok Fresh bean curds stir-fried in spice mixture and chilli pepper, sweet green pepper and coconut milk.

Orak arik Shredded cabbage, chopped onion, shrimp, stir-fried with beaten eggs garnished with green onions.

Opor ajam Chicken pieces fried in curry spice mixture and simmered in coconut milk flavoured with lemon juice.

Opor atal Chicken baked with spices in thick coconut milk.

Oseng-oseng wortel dan bloemkool Carrots and cauliflower stir-fried with garlic, scallions, soy and chili pepper.

Pais ikan   Conger eels spiced with mixture of garlic, shallots, chillis, soy, lemon juice and curry, baked.

Pangal bungkis   Spiced fish steamed in banana leaf.

Pangek ikan   Trout layered with fiddleheads (ferns) flavoured with chillis, shallots, garlic, ginger and curry spices, simmered.

Panggang bandeng   Marinated fish baked with soy, lemon juice, sugar and butter.

Panggang ikan bawal djawa   Fish marinated in paste of garlic and soy grilled and served with sauce of ground chillis, butter, lemon juice and garlic.

Pangsiet   Flour skins filled with ground pork, flavoured with ginger and spices, deep-fried and served in a sweet-sour sauce.

Pastei galigny   Flour skins filled with ground pork and eggs highly seasoned, deep-fried.

Perkedel   Fried or barbecued meat patties spiced with chillis.

Petjel   Small separate heaps of braised vegetables – shredded cabbage, spinach, diced choko, sliced potatoes – and hard-boiled eggs arranged on a plate and served with petjel sauce in a separate bowl; petjel sauce is a paste of fried peanuts, chilli powder and onion.

Perjedel jagung   Corn fritters flavoured with shrimp paste, garlic, chillis and coriander powder, deep-fried.

Petjel ajam   Chicken pieces deep-fried and simmered in sambal badjak (chilli and onion paste), coconut milk, shrimp paste, ginger, garlic and lemon juice.

Petjel terong   Deep-fried aubergine slices in sauce of vinegar, sambal badjak (chilli and onion paste), peanut butter and coconut milk.

Pindang telor   Hardboiled eggs simmered in sauce of onion, garlic and lemon grass.

Pisang goreng   Bananas covered in batter and fried in butter.

Rempah   Patties of minced beef, grated coconut, garlic, egg and coriander, fried.

Rempeyek   Patties of crushed peanuts, onion, garlic, rice flour and spices, deep-fried.

Rendang   Beef slices simmered in savoury sauce of ginger, onion, garlic, chillis and coconut milk, cooked until sauce is dry and the meat is coated a dark brown.

Roti djalah   Lacy, holey pancakes.

Roti koekoes   Steamed cakes of sugar, eggs and flour served dribbled with butter and sprinkled with baker's sugar.

Rudjak   Salad of mixed vegetables or fruit served with a savoury dressing of chillis, sugar, fish paste and lemon juice.

Sajoer   Mixed vegetables and prawns simmered in coconut milk flavoured with garlic, ginger and shrimp paste.

Sajor kerry   Beef cubes, potatoes and cabbage simmered in coconut milk flavoured with spice mixture.

Sajor lodeh   Vegetables in season simmered in coconut broth seasoned with chopped onion, cloves, dried shrimp paste, tamarind pulp and vinegar.

Sajor tjampoer   Shrimp and pork balls in pork broth flavoured with ginger and garlic with additions of celery, cabbage, snow peas and green onions served over steamed rice and onion flakes.

Sajur asam   Spicy vegetable soup.

Sajur bajam   Spicy shrimp paste-flavoured spinach and corn soup.

Sajur bobor   Spicy vegetable soup in broth of coconut milk.

Sajur kare Vegetable mixture (carrots, cabbage, potatoes) curry in coconut broth, flavoured with garlic and lemon grass.

Sajur lemeng Vegetables simmered in curry sauce flavoured with shrimp paste and prawns, thickened with flaked coconut.

Sajur lodeh Vegetable soup in coconut milk with chillis and spices.

Sajur terung atau labu Aubergine or marrow in coconut milk with spices and chillis.

Sambal Side dishes of fiery sauces eaten as complements to the main dish.

Sambal badjak A basic hot sauce of chilli peppers, onions and spice mixture often used as a flavouring agent in many dishes.

Sambal bubuk dari katjang Paste of peanuts, chillis and citrus leaf.

Sambal goreng hati Liver pieces stir-fried in paste of onion, garlic, chilli and trasi (fermented shrimp or prawn paste) then simmered in coconut milk until sauce thickens.

Sambal goreng kering Boiled beef strips stir-fried with sweet pepper strips flavoured with shrimp paste and garlic.

Sambal goreng lombok idjo Sweet green peppers stir-fried with chillis, garlic and soy bean paste.

Sambal goreng pedas Prawns stir-fried with chillis, garlic and onions, simmered in coconut milk and lemon juice.

Sambal goreng sajuran Vegetable mix fried in chilli-based paste and simmered in coconut milk.

Sambal goreng telor Hardboiled eggs simmered in sauce of chillis, onions, ground nuts and coconut milk.

Sambal goreng tomaat Unripe tomatoes and fresh shrimp stir-fried with sambal badjak (chilli and onion paste), simmered in coconut milk and spices.

Sambal goreng udang Prawns stir-fried in chillis and spices, simmered in coconut milk, lemon juice and tamarind water.

Sambal goreng udang dan telur Prawns and hardboiled eggs stir-fried in spicy sauce, served with fresh tomatoes.

Sambal kelapa Grated coconut flavoured with chillis, garlic and lemon juice.

Sambal oedang Prawns in sweet-sour sauce with chillis and ginger, simmered in coconut milk.

Sambal tempeh Soy bean curd baked until hard, flavoured with chillis and dried shrimp paste.

Sambal terasi or blacan Condiment paste of chillis, brown sugar, lemon juice, shallots and garlic.

Sate ajam Boned chicken breast cubes marinated in soy and garlic, skewered and grilled served with a peanut butter, chilli, ground nut and coconut milk sauce.

Sate babi Pork cubes marinated in a sauce of soy, garlic, cloves and brown sugar, grilled over a charcoal fire.

Sate bandeng Elaborate fish dish in which the fish is boned and restuffed with its meat flavoured with spices and onion, wrapped in foil and grilled or baked.

Sate bumbu Beef cubes simmered in curry-flavoured sauce, skewered and grilled over charcoal fire.

Sate kambing Lamb cubes marinated in soy, garlic and chillis, skewered and grilled over charcoal fire and served with sauce of peanut butter, garlic and shrimp paste.

Sate kambing mumbu ketjap Mutton or lamb cubes marinated in soy and garlic, skewered and grilled over charcoal fire served with a sauce of chopped onion, chillis, ground nuts and lemon juice.

Sate koening Beef cubes marinated in coconut milk, curry spices, sambal badjak (chilli and onion paste), skewered and grilled over charcoal fire.

Sate padang Sumatra-style skewered cubes of heart, liver or tripe simmered in paste of chillis, onions, garlic and ginger grilled and served with cooking liquid.

Sate udang Prawns marinated in shrimp paste and coconut milk, grilled.

Saus kacang Condiment of ground peanuts, shrimp paste, sambal badjak and coconut milk.

Sayur lemak Vegetable marrows and potatoes simmered in chillis, ginger, beef stock and coconut milk.

Sayur lodeh jakarta Aubergines, bamboo shoots and cabbage simmered in coconut milk, garlic and chillis.

Semur daging Beef cubes simmered in soy, ginger, onion and lemon.

Sercending Condiment of roasted coconuts, ground peanuts, garlic, shrimp paste and curry spices.

Serundeng A garnish of grated coconut, cumin, garlic, ginger, lemon juice and ground peanuts.

Serigaja Pudding of coconut milk, eggs and sugar.

Singgang ajam Trussed chicken marinated in paste of chillis, ginger and garlic, simmered in coconut milk, then grilled.

Soto ajam Chicken simmered in flavoured broth served garnished with hardboiled eggs, cabbage, potatoes; this is a basic soup and there are many variations depending upon the availability of vegetables and the whim of the cook.

Soto bandung Tripe simmered in broth served with braised turnips and scallions garnished with onion flakes and fried lima beans condimented with sambal sauce and ground nut paste.

Soto danging Beef soup flavoured with prawns, onions, garlic and ginger.

Soto ikan Fish soup with potatoes, onions and carrots, flavoured with chilli and turmeric in coconut milk served with vermicelli.

Tahu ketjap Fried bean curds and hardboiled eggs served with a sauce of soy, shrimp paste and sambal badjak (chilli and onion paste).

Tahu goreng ketjap Fried bean curds covered with bean sprouts and cucumbers with sauce of soy, garlic, onion and chillis poured over all.

Tahu pong Bean curd omelette flavoured with soy and peanut paste.

Tumis Vegetables in season stir-fried with chillis, garlic and soy.

Tumis buncis Green beans simmered in broth flavoured with spices and chillis.

Urap Green vegetables served in a spicy coconut sauce.

Useful words

Ketjap Soy sauce.
Lombok Chilis.
Sambal ulek Chili paste.
Santan kental Coconut milk.
Tahu Bean curd.
Tauco Salted bean flavouring.

JAPAN

Aburage Deep-fried bean curds.

Aegoromo Sauce of white soy bean paste, sweet rice wine, sesame oil, sugar and white vinegar to accompany cooked vegetables such as green beans, asparagus, cauliflower and broccoli.

Aji no kara-age Mackerel coated in flour and deep-fried, soaked in vinegar and sugar mixture then served with par-boiled bean sprouts, grated Japanese radish sprinkled with cayenne pepper.

Aji no nitsuke Sprats or herrings simmered in soy sauce and ginger.

Aji no shisoage Mackerel ground into paste with sweet rice wine, sake and sugar wrapped in leaves and deep-fried.

Ajitsuke tempura Konnyaku (tuber root cake), chicken breasts and bamboo shoots marinated in soy and sweet rice wine, coated in tempura batter and deep-fried, served with dipping sauce of dashi, soy and sweet rice wine.

Aka karashisumiso Sauce of red soy bean paste, sugar, rice wine, mustard and vinegar used as a dip for raw vegetables.

Aki tsuki Chicken, noodle and egg dish flavoured with caviar and served in chicken broth.

Amazake Sweet sake (rice wine).

Anago mushi An arrangement of eels, mushrooms, kamaboko (fish sausage), lily root and lemon peel over which is poured eggs mixed with chicken broth, baked until eggs are set into custard.

Arare Crisp cocktail crackers of rice flour.

Asuka nabe A stew usually of chicken with shirataki (bean thread noodles) and vegetables in chicken broth.

Asuparagasu to sumiso Boiled asparagus served with a dipping sauce of soy bean paste, vinegar and sugar.

Awabi no sumashi Abalone soup with tofu, lemon slivers and spinach garnish.

Ayu shio-yaki Trout rubbed with salt and grilled served with vinegar and dashi (basic soup stock) sauce.

Botan-nabe Thin slices of boar meat (a delicacy in Japan), tofu, burdock root, spring onions and bean thread noodles arranged on a platter and cooked at the table in chicken stock flavoured with sake and white bean paste.

Buta ashi no mizuni Pork shank simmered in broth flavoured with sherry, ginger, leeks, lemon rind and served on a bed of braised Swiss chard with thickened cooking liquid poured over all.

Buta kiki no isobe age Ground pork mixture rolled in seaweed then coated in flour and egg and deep-fried.

Buta kiku no mushini Pork loin simmered in broth flavoured with sake, ginger, onions served with boiled asparagus, broccoli or cauliflower and dipping sauce of white soy bean paste, egg yolks, sake, sugar, vinegar and mustard.

Buta no hikiniku no mochigomemashi Ground pork balls flavoured with ginger, sake, minced dried mushrooms, coated with sweet rice mixture and steamed served with mustard and soy sauce.

Buta no kagoshima Boneless pork roast marinated in mixture of miso, sake, sugar and soy, then roasted in oven, served with cooking liquid gravy.

Buta no mizutaki Bite-size pork pieces arranged on a platter with tofu, mushrooms, lettuce, radish strips, bean sprouts and dried kelp cooked at the table in boiling water by the diner and eaten dipped in sauce of grated ginger, soy and lemon juice.

Buta teriyaki Pork cubes marinated in teriyaki sauce (soy, sake, sugar) skewered and grilled on open fire.

Buta to zucchini okazu Pork slices stir-fried with zucchini (courgettes), onions and tomatoes flavoured with soy sauce.

Butadofu Pork strips stir-fried with mushrooms, water chestnuts, onion in sauce of sugar, soy bean paste, ginger and soy then simmered with tofu cubes.

Butanabe Thin slices of pork, cabbage and tofu cooked at the table in seaweed broth (or basic chicken broth) and dipped in vinegar, ginger and grated radish sauce.

Cashew nuts no otsumami Cashew nuts stir-fried with garlic, soy, miso and sugar.

Chanko nabe Chicken stew with mushrooms, bean curd, bean thread noodles, bamboo shoots, carrots, cabbage and leeks.

Chawan mushi Chicken slices, fish cake slices steamed in egg custard garnished with shrimp and minced mushrooms.

Chikuzenni Chicken pieces, carrots, mushrooms and potatoes, cooked in chicken broth flavoured with soy and sugar until most of the liquid is absorbed by the meat and vegetables.

Chimaki Rice dumplings wrapped in bamboo leaves and steamed.

Chirashizushi A rice salad in which various ingredients such as shrimps, bamboo shoots, peas, lotus root and fried egg strips are mixed with prepared sushi rice (rice flavoured with vinegar and sugar).

Chirinabe Fish slices and vegetables such as mushrooms, cabbage, bamboo shoots cooked in broth at the table by the diner and eaten dipped in soy and ginger sauce.

Coconut mochi Coconut sweet-rice flour cake topped with sesame seeds.

Daikon namasu Japanese radish and carrot strips marinated in salt and served with a sauce of vinegar and sugar.

Daikon no Hawaii zuke Hawaiian-style pickles in which radish is cured in salt and packed in sugar and vinegar mixture.

Dashi A broth made of katsuobushi (dried bonito shavings) and kombu (dried kelp) used as a base for soups and sauces and as a stock for many simmered dishes.

Dashi maki tamago Thin egg omelette flavoured with dashi and soy, served cut into thin strips or used as garnish in many dishes.

Dobin mushi 'Mushrooms in a teapot'—mushrooms, chicken breasts, prawns simmered in dashi in an earthenware teapot and brought to the table where the broth is drunk from tea bowls and the food morsels served in them as a second course.

Dobozuke Fermented rice for pickling cucumbers.

Donburi Means 'big bowl' and is hot rice topped with various fish, meats, eggs or vegetables—a meal-in-one dish popular for lunch: **katsudon** hot rice topped with leftover pieces of pork or lamb cutlet warmed in dashi broth with onions; **kitsune** hot rice topped with fried bean curds and spring onions flavoured with soy and wine in dashi broth; **oyaki** hot rice topped with a mixture of chicken breast, bamboo shoots, kamaboko (fish cake), dried mushrooms simmered in soy and mixed with egg; **tanin** hot rice topped with spring onions stir-fried with beef strips; **tekkadon** hot rice topped with nori (dried seaweed) sheet strips and tuna fillets; **tendon** hot rice topped with shrimp tempura; **unagi** hot rice topped with eels simmered in dashi and sweet rice wine; **yakitori** hot rice topped with fried chicken

Dotenabe Raw oysters, clams, prawns or other shellfish, bean curd, spring onions, spinach or chrysanthemum leaves, shirataki noodles (yam noodles) are brought to the table and cooked in dashi stock flavoured with miso (white bean paste) and the diners help themselves to the food in the simmering pot.

Genghis khan Beef slices marinated in soy, sake and minced leeks stir-fried with mushrooms, onions, aubergines and green peppers—cooked at the table in a special frying pan so that meat and vegetables are just barely done; served with soy and grated horseradish or dashi with soy and sesame seeds.

Gobo maki Burdock roots boiled in vinegar and sugar and tied in bundles with marinated beef strips, broiled.

Goma dare Sauce of crushed sesame seeds, soy, sweet rice wine and soy bean paste, served with grilled beef dishes.

Goma yaki Chicken breasts skinned and boned, marinated in rice wine, soy, vinegar and crushed sesame seeds then grilled over high heat, served with lemon wedges and spring onions.

Gomoku gohan Rice cooked with a mixture of chicken meat, burdock root, mushroom, carrot sticks and deep-fried soy bean curd, simmered in soy and mirin.

Gomoku soba Rice noodles served in a broth with marinated pork strips, garnished with carrot and egg omelette strips.

Gyoza Flour dumplings stuffed with a mixture of ground pork, chopped cabbage, onion, bamboo shoot, mushroom, ginger and soy, fried and then simmered in broth.

Gyu reba no itameni Sliced beef or calves liver marinated in soy and sweet rice wine then stir-fried with chopped onion, garlic, ginger and red pepper.

Gyuniku no amiyaki Beef steaks marinated in soy and sake grilled and served with soy, red pepper and grated ginger.

Gyuniku no kushiyaki Beef and onion cubes skewered and marinated in soy and rice wine, dipped in flour and beaten egg and deep-fried.

Gyuniku no yawatamaki Burdock root strips rolled in beef slices, browned then simmered in sauce of soy, sugar, sake.

Gyuniku to yasai no itamemono Beef strips rolled in flour and quick-fried combined with stir-fried green peppers, mushrooms, carrots and bean sprouts flavoured lightly with soy, garnished with egg omelette strips.

Hakusai nabe Chinese cabbage and mixed vegetable stew garnished with prawns and ham.

Hamaguri Clams.

Hamaguri no karayaki Fresh clams dipped in egg white, broiled and flavoured with soy and sake.

Hamaguri to shiitake ushiojiru Fresh clam broth with mushrooms and spinach flavoured with lemon served with the cooked clams.

Harusame Soup in which diner adds ingredients at the table into the basic stock of dashi or chicken broth – bean threads, mushrooms, prawns, burdock root, onions, carrots, cucumbers, etc are arranged on a platter to be dipped into the stock according to individual taste.

Hijiki to aburage Seaweed simmered in dashi with soy and sweet wine combined with fried bean curds.

Hirame Flat fish, halibut.

Hiyamugi Medium-size wheat noodles served cold with ice cubes and garnished with shrimps, mushrooms and egg omelette strips with a sauce of soy, wine and bonito flakes.

Hiyashi gomoku-soba Buckwheat noodles served cold garnished with ham strips, cucumbers, mushrooms and egg omelette strips served with dashi and soy.

Horaku yaki Fish lightly salted and baked with mushrooms, prawns and chestnuts on a bed of pine needles.

Horenso no goma-ae Parboiled spinach dressed with ground sesame seeds and soy sauce.

Horenso no shiro-ae Freshly cooked spinach and konnyaku (tuber root cake commonly known as devil's tongue) served with a dressing of ground sesame seeds, tofu and bean paste.

Horenso tamago maki Spinach rolled in egg sheets and served sliced so that the green vegetable is surrounded by a circle of yellow; eaten with a soy sauce dip.

Ichiban dashi Basic soup stock or sauce base of dried kelp (kombu) and dried bonito shavings (katsuobushi).

Ika Squid.

Ika no mirinyaki Squid marinated in soy and rice wine, grilled.

Imo Potato.

Inarizushi Fried bean curd pouches filled with flavoured rice mixed with carrot slivers, mushroom pieces and burdock root.

Ingen no aemono Green beans dressed with soy, rice wine and grated ginger root.

Ingenmame French or kidney bean.

Iridori Chicken stewed with onions, carrots, mushrooms, bamboo shoots and taro root, flavoured with soy, ginger and wine.

Iriko Small dried sardines.

Iritsukedofu Bean curds and eggs heated until eggs are set, flavoured with fish flakes and soy sauce.

Ise-ebi Lobster.

Ishikari nabe A one-pot dish of salmon with mushrooms, spinach, cabbage, chrysanthemum leaves and bean curd.

Kabayaki Grilled eel flavoured with soy and rice wine.

Kabocha Japanese pumpkin cut into cubes and simmered in broth of dashi, sugar, rice wine with dried seaweed.

Kabu no suzuke Turnips salted and pickled in vinegar, sugar, red pepper and dried kelp.

Kabuto yaki Named after the dome-shaped grill in which the food is cooked, said to resemble the helmets worn by Genghis Khan's soldiers; thinly sliced lamb or mutton arranged on a platter with potatoes, bell peppers, onion, carrots, aubergine, usually brought to the table and there grilled by the diner, served with a dipping sauce of soy bean paste, sesame seeds, vinegar.

Kai gohan Rice cooked with clams in the shell flavoured with rice wine and soy.

Kai no misoni Fresh clams stir-fried with garlic, sake, red soy bean paste and sugar.

Kakejiru Basic soup stock for noodles consisting of dashi, soy and rice wine.

Kaki Persimmons.

Kaki no irini Fresh oysters stir-fried with onions, garlic and ginger in sauce of soy, sake, sugar.

Kaki no miso shiru Soup of basic dashi stock with oysters, flavoured with white or red soy bean paste and grated ginger.

Kakiage Tempura (batter fried food) of shrimps, mushrooms, green beans, shredded carrots or green peas.

Kakimeshi Rice cooked with sake and seaweed with addition of fresh oysters to steam in cooked rice.

Kakitama jiru Soup of dashi stock thickened with beaten eggs garnished with snow peas.

Kamasu teriyaki Barracuda steaks marinated in soy and rice wine grilled over charcoal or broiled.

Kamo no tsukiyaki Duck pieces marinated in soy, sherry and ginger, stir-fried with mushrooms and onions, simmered in marinade liquid.

Kamoboko Fish sausage of pounded whitefish, cornflour and rice wine used in soups and casseroles; often dyed pink or green.

Kani gohan Rice cooked in dashi stock mixed with crab, soy and rice wine served garnished with egg omelette strips.

Kani no ginshiyaki Crab baked with aubergine and mushrooms flavoured with sake.

Kani to kyuri namasu Crab and cucumber salad dressed with vinegar, soy and rice wine.

Karashi joyu Dipping sauce of soy and hot mustard.

Karashi mayonnaise Dipping sauce of mayonnaise and hot mustard.

Karashina no shiozuke Pickled mustard leaves.

Katsudon Basic rice dish topped with pieces of lamb or pork, with dashi stock, soy and wine sauce poured over all.

Katsuobushi Dried bonito – the basic ingredient of dashi or Japanese soup stock used as a base for soups and sauces.

Katsutera Sponge cake.

Kenchin jiru Soup of basic dashi stock with bean curd, burdock root strips, mushrooms, boned chicken slivers, radish and carrot strips flavoured with soy and pepper; an elaborate soup almost a meal in itself.

Kiji Pheasant.

Kimini Prawns simmered in dashi, soy and sake covered with beaten egg yolks.

Kimpira Burdock root strips stir-fried in soy and wine.

Kimo Liver.

Kimo no iritsuke Chicken livers marinated in soy, garlic and ginger, sautéed and served with thickened marinade liquid.

Kimo no tsukeage Chicken livers marinated in soy, ginger and sake, coated with batter and deep-fried.

Kinoko Mushroom.

Kinome no takenoki yaki Bamboo shoots sautéed in soy and wine.

Kinomeae Bamboo shoots and squid salad dressed with a sauce of spinach leaves, soy, wine, white bean paste and dashi.

Kinton Dried lima beans cooked with sugar and sake served as a side dish.

Kitsune donburi Basic rice dish topped with strips of aburage (fried bean curd), spring onions with sauce of dashi, soy and wine poured over all.

Kitsune soba   Buckwheat noodles with aburage (fried bean curd) in dashi stock, soy and wine.

Kitsune udon   Wide wheat flour noodles topped with aburage and spring onions in dashi stock.

Ko ebi   Shrimp.

Kohitsuji   Lamb.

Koi   Carp.

Kombu   Seaweed kelp.

Konnyaku   (Devil's tongue jelly) – powdered tuber roots formed into chewy cakes often used as an ingredient in casseroles to add texture interest.

Konnyaku no irini   Boiled devil's tongue jelly stir-fried with red chilli pepper, sugar, sake and soy garnished with sesame seeds.

Konnyaku no misoni   Devil's tongue jelly boiled and stir-fried in sauce of dashi, white soy bean paste and sake garnished with seaweed flakes.

Koshian   Red bean paste used as a basic flavouring ingredient.

Koushi   Veal.

Koya mushi   Steamed egg custard with bean curds, scallops, mushrooms and spinach leaves mixed in dashi stock.

Kuri gohan   Rice cooked with chestnuts flavoured with wine, dried kelp and sesame seeds.

Kuri kinton   Mashed sweet potatoes and chestnuts flavoured with sugar and rice wine.

Kuri no shibukawani   Chestnuts cooked in sauce of sugar, rice wine and soy eaten as a side dish.

Kuromame   Black Oriental beans cooked in sugar syrup for three consecutive days until beans are almost solidified then cooked with soy and chestnuts to be eaten as a condiment with rice and other dishes.

Kuzuhiki   Basic dashi soup with tofu.

Kyuri matsumae   Cucumbers pickled in soy sauce.

Kyuri no misozume   Fresh hollowed cucumbers stuffed with a paste of soy bean, ginger and sake served cut into rounds.

Kyuri to kani no sunomono   Crab and cucumber salad dressed with sugar and rice vinegar garnished with lemon slices and sesame seed.

Kyuri to wakame sunomono   Cucumber and seaweed salad dressed with dried white fish soaked in vinegar, sugar and soy sauce.

Maguro   Tunnyfish.

Manju   Steamed buns filled with sugared crushed red beans.

Masai no yasai zume   Rainbow trout cavity stuffed with slivered bamboo shoots, mushrooms and carrots, flavoured with soy and wine and baked.

Masu no ginshiyaki   Trout salted and marinated in sake wrapped in foil with lemon and baked.

Match kinton   Mashed sweet potato flavoured with green tea.

Matsutake gohan   Rice cooked with mushrooms flavoured with seaweed, soy and sake.

Matsutake tsutsumi yaki   Mushrooms grown in pine forests considered a delicacy with a unique flavour and crispness of texture; a simple dish is to wrap them in aluminium foil to broil with a sauce of soy, rice wine and lemon juice.

Mattcha aisu kurimu   Green tea ice cream.

Mattcha mochi   Rice cake flavoured with green tea.

Maze gohan   Rice cooked with peas, carrots and shrimps, flavoured with ginger, gingko nuts, soy and sake.

Menrui The generic name for noodles eaten either hot or cold – an omnipresent food in Japan.

Mi iro gohan 'Three-coloured-rice' – rice with peas and beef.

Mikan Tangerine.

Miso shiru A basic soup of miso, a fermented mixture of soy beans and malted rice.

Mitsumame Almond-flavoured milk jelly served with fruit topping.

Mitzutaki Chicken pieces, tofu and a selection of vegetables arranged on a platter and brought to the table to be cooked in simmering stock after which diners help themselves to the food, dipping them in a selection of sauces; vegetables usually include Chinese cabbage, mushrooms, bamboo shoots and onion.

Mizuyokan Jelly of agar agar served with sugared crushed red beans.

Momiji oroshi A dipping sauce of grated daikon (Japanese radish) and chilli pepper.

Momo Peach.

Moyashi Bean sprouts.

Moyashi no okazu Bean sprouts stirred into a mixture of pork and tofu cooked with soy and dashi.

Moyashi sunomono A salad of parboiled bean sprouts dressed with vinegar, soy, sesame oil and ginger.

Moyashi to tori aemono A salad of bean sprouts, shredded chicken meat and celery dressed with dashi, vinegar, white soy bean paste, peanut butter and soy garnished with sesame seeds.

Mushi awabi Abalone steamed with sake sliced thinly and served with cucumber slices garnished with lemon.

Nabeyaki udon Broad noodles in broth with chicken strips, spring onions, topped with raw egg which cooks in the hot broth.

Nagasaki yakiniku Beef slices marinated in red bean paste, soy and sesame oil, fried.

Namasu Fish salad.

Namako no oroshi suae Sliced sea cucumbers served with grated Japanese radish and ginger in rice vinegar, soy and lemon juice.

Namazake no ginshiyaki Salmon steaks topped with onion rings and lemon slices, wrapped in foil and baked.

Nana iro namasu Rainbow salad of shirataki (yam noodles), Japanese radish, carrot, cucumber, tomato and kamaboko (fish cake), dressed with lemon juice, wine, sugar and sesame seeds.

Nappa no okazu Cabbage stir-fried with pork strips and soy served with hot mustard and soy sauce.

Nasu Aubergine.

Nasu no dengaku Aubergine slices fried and broiled with a topping of bean paste, soy, sake, wine and sesame seed mixture.

Nasu no karashizuke Aubergines pickled in soy, sugar, white soy bean paste, dry mustard and sake.

Nasu no miso Aubergines filled with beef, pork, shrimps, spring onions and deep-fried.

Nasu no misoitame Aubergine slices deep-fried combined with stir-fried ground pork, celery, mushrooms, chilli pepper rings, served with a sauce of red bean paste, sake, soy and sugar.

Nasu shigiyaki Aubergine slices brushed with mixture of red bean paste, sugar, rice wine and dashi, grilled.

Nasu to aburage no nibitashi Parboiled aubergine slices combined with fried bean curd cooked in soy, dashi and sugar dressed with mustard, soy, garnished with shiso (green beefsteak leaves).

Nasu to edamame goma ae Boiled aubergine slices combined with boiled soy beans dressed with soy, dashi and sesame seeds.

Negi shigiyaki Leeks covered with mixture of red bean paste, sugar, sweet rice wine and dashi, grilled.

Nibe no yakimono Sea bass steaks fried with lemon slices and served with a sauce of grated Japanese radish and soy.

Nigiri zushi Flavoured rice ovals topped with tuna or sea bass pieces or shrimps or egg omelette strips—a snack food.

Niku Meat.

Niku dango Pork and beef balls stir-fried with chopped ginger and garlic, simmered in dashi broth.

Niku no miso yaki Beef slices marinated in bean paste, soy, sugar, ginger and scallions, stir-fried with marinade liquid.

Nimono Fish and fowl cooked with mushrooms, bamboo shoots and carrots in broth of soy, dashi and rice wine.

Ninjin Carrot.

Niwatori Chicken.

Nizakana Fresh salmon slices simmered with onion in a sauce of sake, soy, sugar and ginger root.

Noppei jiru A hearty vegetable soup of dashi stock, radishes, carrots, turnips, kidney beans, fried bean curds and mushrooms.

Nori Black seaweed—often dried into thin sheets used as a cover for sushi rolls or crumbled into soups and casseroles as a flavouring agent.

Nori chazuke Cooked rice in a bowl of green tea topped with a piece of crumbled dry seaweed—taken as a snack.

Norimaki Flavoured rice roll with inner core of fish, mushrooms, egg strips and gourd shavings, covered with black dried seaweed sheet, sliced into cylinders.

Nuka no tsukemono Vegetable pickle cured in rice bran.

Nuta Salad of clams marinated in vinegar combined with parboiled spring onions dressed with sake, bean paste and wine.

Nuta negi Spring onions and scallops served in a sauce of bean paste, dashi, vinegar and dry mustard.

Oboro Hot rice topped with chicken pieces, peas and mushrooms moistened with dashi stock and soy sauce.

Odamaki mushi Egg custard containing chicken pieces, mushrooms, spinach, lily root, kamoboko (fish cake) and prawns, served with udon noodles as a base.

Oden A hearty combination of ingredients in broth—two types of bean curd, Japanese radish, cabbage, kamoboko (fish cake), konnyaku (tuber root cake), carrot, squid, hard-boiled eggs combined in broth flavoured with soy and rice wine.

Ohagi Sweet rice cakes covered with sweetened mashed red bean paste.

Okara no irini A casserole of deep-fried soy bean cakes, carrot sticks, mushrooms, konnyaku (tuber root cakes), slivered burdock roots and soy bean curd whey seasoned with soy, sugar, sake and dashi.

Okashi Sweets usually eaten for snacks or with tea; dessert is usually fresh fruit in season.

Okayu Soft rice cooked in more than normal amount of water rendering the rice almost mushy for easy digestion.

Okoshi Sweet puffed rice squares.

Omoyu Rice milk – liquid from rice cooked in abundant water.

Onigiri Rice balls into which are pressed fish slices, rolled in toasted, crushed sesame seeds.

Oroshi dare Dipping sauce of grated Japanese radish, grated ginger, rice vinegar, soy and green onion.

Osaka kitsune udon Wide noodles in broth topped with fried bean curd strips, boned chicken pieces and mushrooms.

Oshi sushi Flavoured rice pressed in wooden moulds topped with a variety of vegetables and meat or fish, served cut into small pieces, an ideal *hors-d'oeuvre* or picnic food.

Oyako domburi Hot rice topped with sliced chicken meat, egg strips and spring onions.

Oyako zosui Rice cooked with boned sliced chicken in dashi stock flavoured with soy to which beaten eggs are added just before serving.

Ozoni Soup of dashi stock with mochi (small rice flour cakes), kamoboko (fish cake) slices, shrimp and cabbage or spinach.

Rakkyo no amazuzuke Salted scallion pickles with chilli peppers.

Remon Lemon.

Renkon Lotus root.

Ringo Apple.

Saba no karaage no suzuke Mackerel coated with flour and deep-fried then simmered in dashi, soy and wine with addition of grated radish.

Saba no nitsuke Oily fish such as mackerel, tuna, turbot simmered in water flavoured with sugar, rice wine, sake, soy.

Saba no sutataki Mackerel salted then marinated in mixture of vinegar and sugar until flesh whitens, then served with strips of carrots, Japanese radish and ginger with vinegar.

Sakana Fish.

Sakana karaage Fish coated with corn flour and deep fried served with sauce of dashi, soy and rice wine.

Sakana miso yaki Oily fish such as mackerel, bonito, tuna, simmered in water, sake and sugar and served covered with sauce of cooking liquid to which is added bean paste (miso) and soy.

Sakana misozuke Fish cured in bean paste mixture and grilled.

Sakana no abura kake Red snapper fillets simmered in water and served with a sauce of soy, ginger and chopped onions with hot oil poured over all just before serving.

Sakana no ginshiyaki Fish baked in foil with mushrooms, gingko nuts and lemon.

Sakana shio yaki Fish grilled with salt.

Sakana uniyaki Fish grilled brushed with chestnut sauce and egg yolk.

Sakana ushiojiru Fish consommé lightly seasoned with soy, sake.

Sake Rice wine – the national drink of Japan.

Sake niwatori Chicken cubes marinated in sake, then poached, served with a sauce of vinegar, sugar and mustard.

Sake no miso yaki Salmon steaks broiled with brushing of white soy bean paste, sugar and soy sauce.

Sashimi The best part of the freshest of prime fish sliced in thin slivers and eaten raw with a sauce of grated Japanese radish, horseradish and soy; the most common sashimi fish are sea-bream, tuna, sole, smelt, cuttlefish, turbot, halibut, abalone and trout.

Sashimi to kyuri Raw fish marinated in salt served rolled in thin slices of salted cucumber.

Satsuma jiru Soup of dashi broth flavoured with red bean paste garnished with chicken and mushrooms.

Saya endo to tofu Pork strips stir-fried with mushrooms, bean curds, onions, snow peas and water chestnuts flavoured with soy and cooking juices thickened with flour.

Seimbei Rice cakes.

Sekihan Red beans cooked with mochi rice (sticky rice) flavoured with salt and sesame seeds, garnished with parsley.

Shabu-shabu An arrangement of beef slices and vegetables such as mushrooms, spring onions, Chinese cabbage, bamboo shoots and bean curds brought to the table for each diner to dip pieces of meat or vegetable in boiling stock of dashi or chicken broth flavoured with soy, red peppers, lemon juice and sesame seeds.

Shichimi togarashi Seven-flavours spice—a blend of pepper leaf, poppy seed, rape seed, hemp seed, dried tangerine peel, chilli and sesame seed.

Shinjagaimo to butaniku no nitsuke Pork cubes simmered with new potatoes in broth of dashi, soy, sugar and ginger.

Shirataki Noodles made of tuber root.

Shiro ae Salad of konnyaku (tuber root cake) pieces, bean curd and carrot strips in dressing of crushed sesame seeds, sugar and soy.

Shiro karashisumiso A dipping sauce of white soy bean paste, sugar, sweet rice wine, dashi, dry mustard and rice vinegar.

Shoga dare Dipping sauce of grated ginger root, soy, wine.

Shoga meshi Rice cooked in flavouring of soy, sake, kelp (dried seaweed) and fresh ginger.

Shoga no amazuzuke Sliced ginger root pickled in vinegar, sugar and beet juice (for colour).

Shoyu Soy sauce—the most basic of Japanese seasonings.

Shungiku Tender leaves of chrysanthemum frequently used in casserole dishes.

Soba Buckwheat noodles.

Somen Wheat noodles.

Su Japanese rice vinegar.

Suchiro takenoko Bamboo shoots simmered in broth of dashi, soy.

Sugaki Raw oysters served with a sauce of grated Japanese radish, grated ginger, lemon juice and rice vinegar.

Suimono Clear broth of dashi stock sometimes simply garnished with a slice of kamoboko (fish cake) or a piece of bean curd with a slice of lemon floating in each bowl.

Sukiyaki A one-dish meal in which thin slices of beef or chicken are arranged on a platter with shirataki (yam noodles), sliced onions, chrysanthemum leaves, mushrooms, bamboo shoots, bean curd and brought to the table to be cooked over a portable stove, seasoned to taste with soy, sake and sugar; diners help themselves to the food dipping it first in raw beaten egg which serves to cool the morsel of food.

Sumashi kiru Chicken soup with udon noodles.

Sushi A generic name for many varieties of dishes in which flavoured rice is shaped or rolled in easily handled sizes and topped with titbits of fish, vegetables, meat or pickles.

Tai shio yaki Whole sea bream generously sprinkled with salt and grilled over charcoal or in broiler.

Taka no kitata Octopus boiled in water and sake and served with dipping sauce of white soy bean paste, soy and vinegar.

Takenoko kimpira Bamboo shoot slices braised in soy, sweet wine, sugar and dash of red pepper.

Takenoko meshi Rice cooked with bamboo shoots in dashi stock flavoured with soy and sake.

Takiawase Minced chicken dumplings (pre-cooked) simmered with bamboo shoots, mushrooms in dashi stock, soy and sugar.

Takuan Japanese radish pickled in salt and rice bran.

Tako no karashimisoae Boiled octopus salad dressed with sugar, vinegar and mustard arranged on platter with cucumber slices and reconstituted dry seaweed.

Tako to kyuri no zensai Boiled octopus pieces skewered with cucumber rings and served with dipping sauce.

Tamago kiru Soup of basic dashi stock into which is poured beaten eggs so they form long strands.

Tamago maki Sweet egg roll.

Tamago zake Egg-nog of sake and honey.

Tanin donburi Hot rice topped with fried marinated beef and onions with dashi sauce poured over all to moisten.

Tarako to tasai no niawase Shirataki (tuber root noodles), cod's roe, leeks and carrots simmered in dashi, soy, sake.

Tazukuri Small dried fish crisped in oven and simmered in sauce of sugar, rice wine and soy.

Tekkadon Hot rice topped with nori (dried seaweed sheet) strips and tuna fillets flavoured with soy.

Tempura Fritters of sea food, vegetables or meat with a crisp batter coating as thin as gauze; the most popular ingredients for tempura are prawns, shrimps, fish, carrot strips, mushrooms, asparagus, parsley, courgettes, aubergines, potatoes, green beans; served with sauce of soy, rice wine and dashi.

Tempura soba Buckwheat noodles in dashi sauce served topped with tempura (seafood or vegetable fritters) or fried fish.

Tendon Tempura pieces served over rice flavoured with dashi, soy.

Tendon donburi Hot rice topped with shrimp tempura with dashi.

Tentsuyu Dipping sauce of dashi, sweet rice wine, soy and grated Japanese radish.

Teppanyaki Mixed grill of any combination of meat or seafood and vegetables cooked at the table for diners to help themselves dipping the morsel into soy and lemon sauce.

Teriyaki gyniku Beef steaks marinated in soy, rice wine, garlic and ginger and quickly browned, served garnished with ginger sprouts or tiny cucumbers marinated in vinegar and soy.

Teriyaki yakiniku Beef slices marinated in dashi, soy and ginger and quickly sautéed.

Tofu Soy bean curd high in protein, calcium and B vitamins, it has the consistency of firm custard, with a bland flavour making it amenable to many uses.

Tofu to hikiniki Soy bean curds stir-fried with minced beef, green peas and onion flavoured with soy, sake and sugar.

Togan shiru Chicken broth mixture of pork strips, mushrooms, water chestnuts and shrimps, poured into hollowed winter melon and baked, garnished with crumbled dry seaweed.

Tori namba soba Buckwheat noodles in broth topped by chicken pieces and spring onions.

Tori namba udon Broad noodles in dashi broth served topped with boned chicken pieces and spring onions.

Tori no kimo tsukudani Chicken livers and leeks simmered in sake, soy, sugar and minced ginger.

Tori no mizutaki Chicken wings, cabbage, soy bean curds and carrots simmered in water; broth is drunk separately and food morsels are dipped in sauce of grated radish, soy and ginger.

Tori no teriyaki Chicken pieces marinated in soy, sherry, garlic and ginger, fried then simmered in marinade.

Tori no yakimeshi Cold rice refried with cooked shredded chicken, celery and onion with egg stirred in.

Tori to mayashi no sumiso ae Shredded cooked chicken breast combined with parboiled bean sprouts dressed with white soy bean paste and mustard.

Torimaki Egg omelette sheet filled with minced chicken.

Toriniku dango no terini Minced chicken balls simmered in broth flavoured with soy, sweet rice wine and sugar.

Toriniku no awayuki age Chicken breast tempura.

Toriniku no nanbanyaki Chicken pieces marinated in basic soy-wine sauce then grilled, brushed with thickened marinade.

Toriniku no shichimi yaki Marinated chicken pieces wrapped in foil and baked.

Toriniku to edo negi Boned chicken cubes rolled in cornflour, stir-fried with leeks then simmered in sauce of soy, sake and ginger.

Toriniku tatsuta age Chicken pieces marinated in soy and wine flavoured with ginger and garlic, rolled in cornflour, deep-fried.

Toriniku to shiitake no teriyaki Thin chicken breast slices in which are wrapped mushrooms, skewered and sautéed in soy and wine.

Tsuke jiru Dipping sauce for noodles – soy, sweet wine, dashi and dried bonito flakes.

Tsukemono Generic name for pickles, an essential accompaniment to every Japanese meal.

Tsukeyaki maguro Tuna steaks marinated in soy, sake, ginger and garlic and grilled.

Tsukeyaki sawara Mackerel marinated in soy, sake, ginger and garlic and grilled.

Tsukimi udon 'Seeing the moon' noodles in broth served with a raw egg (the moon) which cooks from the heat of the broth.

Tsumamimono A generic name for pick-up foods such as *hors d'oeuvres* and picnic foods.

Tsumiire nabe Minced chicken stewed with cabbage rolls, bean curds and leeks in dashi stock.

Umaki Rolled omelette filled with marinated cooked eel.

Umani Boned chicken breasts stewed with burdock root, konnyaku, carrots, bamboo shoots, mushrooms and taro potatoes in dashi stock flavoured with soy.

Umeboshi Pickled sour plums, a popular condiment.

Umeshi Plum wine.

Unagi domburi Hot rice topped with marinated boiled eel moistened with marinade liquid.

Unagi no kabayaki Fish slices marinated in soy and quick-fried.

Udon suki A version of sukiyaki with noodles, clams, chicken and vegetables.

Uno saki Fish version of sukiyaki substituting a variety of fish instead of beef – an arrangement of fish and vegetables cooked at the table.

Ushi ojiru Fish fillets simmered in fish stock and dashi.

Wakame Seaweed.
Wakatakejiru Soup of bamboo shoots and wakame (seaweed) in dashi.
Warabi Edible fern.
Wasabi Horseradish, very strong and green in colour, usually grated and added to dipping sauce.

Yaki matsutake Large fresh mushrooms grilled lightly and served with soy and lemon juice.
Yaki tekenoko Sliced bamboo shoots marinated in soy and rice wine, grilled.
Yakiniku Beef slices and cabbage, onions, sweet potato, bell peppers and mushrooms marinated in soy, vinegar and sugar and grilled.
Yakitori Boned chicken pieces marinated in soy and wine, skewered and grilled served with grated cucumber.
Yakitori donburi Hot rice topped with fried marinated chicken pieces moistened with dashi broth.
Yasai moriawase Mixed vegetables braised with soy, ginger, wine.
Yasai no maki age Aburage (deep-fried bean curd) is filled with marinated, cooked pork strips, mushrooms, bamboo shoots, carrots, and green onions, cooked in soy broth and then fried in deep fat.
Yasai no tempura Tempura (fried fritters) of vegetables – green beans, carrot strips, aubergines, celery, sweet onions, sweet potatoes and white potatoes.
Yokan Sweet made from gelatine and awuki (red bean paste).
Yomogi mochi Green cakes made from sweet (glutinous) rice – flat, round cakes named after the plant which gives it its green colour.
Yosenabe Literally means 'odds and ends' so any combination of fish, meat, noodles and vegetables can be cooked in dashi stock – boned chicken, lean pork, prawns, Chinese cabbage, onions, spinach, carrots, mushrooms, tofu, kamoboko and noodles simmered in dashi stock sprinkled with dash of pepper.
Yudebuta Pork tenderloin simmered in water, soy, ginger root, sliced eaten cold with mustard.
Yudofu Bean curds (tofu), mushrooms, chrysanthemum leaves simmered in stock at the table.

Zenzai Red bean soup with gelatinous rice dumplings (served as a snack).
Zoni Toasted rice cakes served with cooked vegetables and wild duck or chicken.

Useful words

Aemono Salad.
Agemono Food fried in deep oil.
Dango Dumpling, meat ball or croquette.
Dashi Basic Japanese soup stock used in sauces and casseroles.
Kara age Dusting food in cornflour and deep frying.
Kushi age Food skewered and deep-fried.
Menrui Generic name for noodles.
Mirin Sweetened rice wine used as a flavouring agent.
Miso Bean paste used as a flavouring agent.
Misozuke Vegetables pickled in bean paste.
Mushimono Steamed food.

Nabemono Literally 'pot thing' referring to any meal cooked in one pot.

Nimono Boiled food.

Nitsuke Simmering fish or vegetables in soy sauce and sugar.

Okazu Things to eat with rice.

Shojin ryori Buddhist vegetarian cooking.

Shoyu Soy sauce – the most important flavouring agent in Japanese cuisine.

Sunimono 'Vinegared things' – pickles indispensable at every meal.

Teriyaki Grilling foods while basting with soy and rice wine.

Tofu Bean curd.

Tsukeyaki Method of cooking in which fish or meat is marinated in soy and other seasonings then sautéed or grilled.

Yaita Grilled.

Yaki Baking or roasting.

Yakimono Fish and fowl boiled together.

KOREA

Al-sam Minced beef flavoured with soy and scallions folded in egg sheets served with vinegar-soy sauce.

Bintatok Korean pizza – dough of ground mung beans fried on one side, the other topped with onion, pepper and shredded carrot served with hot pepper sauce.

Bulgogi Sliced beef marinated in soy, sesame seeds, sugar, garlic and ginger traditionally braised at the table in special burners.

Cha soh juhn Fritters of potatoes, onions and carrots fried and served with vinegar-soy sauce.

Cha soh kook Vegetable soup of cabbage, carrots, onions and potatoes flavoured with beef strips, soy and sesame seeds.

Chai yuk sang cha Boiled pork strips combined, as in a salad, with separately fried carrot strips, turnips, onions, mushrooms and spinach dressed with soy, sugar, vinegar, garlic and pine nuts.

Chap chee Stir-fried Chinese cabbage, carrot strips, spinach and mushrooms mixed with boiled vermicelli noodles (bean threads), flavoured with sesame seed oil, soy, sugar, sesame seeds.

Cho kai kook Clam soup flavoured with beef and soy.

Cho kanjang Dipping sauce of soy, vinegar, sesame seeds and sugar.

Cho kay tang Soup of chicken broth thickened with mashed sesame seeds flavoured with soy, ginger served with chicken meat strips, fried cucumber, mushrooms, egg omelette strips and pears, served cold.

Cho na mool Salad of braised carrot strips, celery and cabbage dressed with vinegar, sugar and sesame seed oil.

Cho raan Seeded dates coated in cinnamon and sugar, rolled in ground nuts.

Chop chai Chopped marinated beef combined with pork strips, bean sprouts, mushrooms and bean threads flavoured with soy, garlic and sesame seeds garnished with sliced pear and egg strips.

Dak Chicken.

Dak jim Chicken pieces stewed with mushrooms, bamboo shoots, chestnuts and walnuts flavoured with soy, pepper and sesame seeds.

Dal ke hwa chyah Strawberry punch.

Dak kook Chicken soup flavoured with soy, garlic and onion served topped with chicken and egg strips.

Dak kui Chicken pieces marinated in soy, garlic, ginger, sesame oil and broiled.

Dak pok kum Boned chicken pieces cooked in savoury sauce of soy, garlic, onions with addition of mushrooms.

Heen pahb White rice.

Ho pahk jim Squash squares filled with marinated minced beef, chili pepper and egg strips, simmered in broth.

Jang san juk Minced beef squares, highly seasoned with soy, peppers, garlic, eaten as a condiment.

Jeotkal Fish–herring, squid, anchovy–pickled in salt and vinegar and served as a condiment.

Juhn Fritter of vegetable or meat: **gogoo mah** sweet potato; **ho bak** summer squash; **kah ri** aubergine; **ko choo** pepper stuffed with meat; **pah** green onion.

Juhn kol Slivers of tender beef arranged raw with an accompanying selection of vegetables–cabbage, mushrooms, carrots–to be cooked at the table by searing the meat then adding broth in which to cook vegetables ending with an egg steamed for each person.

Ka ri jim Beef ribs boiled with vegetables.

Kah ri juhn Aubergine slices, dipped in flour and egg, fried.

Kah ri kui Grilled pork spare-ribs marinated in soy, ginger, sugar.

Kahn juhn Parboiled liver rolled in flour and egg, fried, served with vinegar-soy sauce.

Kak pab White rice mixed with almonds, walnuts, honey and soy.

Kal bee jim Beef spare-ribs simmered with chestnuts and bamboo shoots in broth flavoured with soy, sesame seed oil, sugar and garlic.

Kam ja juhn Parboiled potatoes coated in flour and egg, fried.

Kan pok kum Liver rolled in flour and egg and fried, served with vinegar-soy sauce.

Ke juhn Fried lobster.

Keen kong na mool String beans cooked and combined with stir-fried beef and flavoured with soy, sesame seed and green onions.

Khong ja pahn Black beans cooked in soy, candied ginger, chilli peppers, sugar and sesame seed until hard and salty, eaten in small amounts with rice.

Khong na mool Salad of bean sprouts dressed with soy, sugar and sesame seeds.

Kim chi Spicy, peppery vegetable pickle served as an accompaniment at all meals: **jahng** with soy sauce base; **moo** turnip; **oi** cucumber (less fiery); **pom** cabbage or turnips (less fiery, in a water base); **tong** cabbage.

Ko chooh juhn Small green peppers filled with minced meat mixture, dipped in flour and egg, fried.

Ko koo mah juhn Cooked sweet potatoes dipped in flour and egg and fried.

Kook Soup, almost always a part of a luncheon or dinner, served hot and well-spiced; **cha-soh** vegetable; **cho-kai** clam; **cho-kay** sesame seed; **dak** chicken; **gool** oyster; **ka-gi** aubergine; **kah-ri** ribs; **kam-ja** potato; **ke-ran** egg; **ko-oum** beef and turnip; **oi** cucumber; **pah** green onion; **paj-hoo** cabbage; **puh-sul** mushroom; **pyun-su** summer meat dumplings; **sang-suhn** fish; **see-kum-chee** spinach; **wan-ja** beef ball.

Kook soo Fine Oriental noodles in a soup base garnished with fried egg strips, marinated beef or pork strips, vegetables such as cucumber strips, green onion, grated turnips, seasoned with soy and pepper sauce.

Kool juhn Oysters dipped in flour and egg and fried.

Koon gogi Beef steak marinated in soy, sugar, garlic, ginger, grilled over charcoal fire.

Ku chul paan Minced beef marinated in soy, sesame seeds, onion and garlic fried and arranged on a platter with a selection of parboiled vegetables such as spinach, cucumber, bean sprouts, carrots, mushrooms and egg strips, to be eaten with flat, flour pancakes rolled by the diner at the table.

Maeum tang Spicy fish soup flavoured with chillis, ginger, garlic, onion served with addition of stir-fried courgettes and green peppers.

Man doo Large dumplings of thin flour pastry filled with spicy, elaborate filling of marinated beef, pork or shrimp or a combination of meats and bean sprouts, marinated cabbage, scallions.

Man do kook Man doo dumplings served in chicken broth garnished with chicken meat strips and egg omelette strips, served with vinegar-soy sauce.

Mill kook soo Wheat flour noodles served in meat broth garnished with marinated and boiled beef slices, egg omelette strips and shredded red pepper.

Mils sam Thin flour pancake strips fried with a parsley or spinach leaf pressed to one side flavoured with cinnamon and sugar.

Moo sang cha Carrot and turnip salad dressed with vinegar and sugar.

Moo sook jang ah gee Turnips cooked with chopped beef flavoured with chillis, soy, garlic and sesame seeds – very hot and spicy.

Na mul Salad – an important element in Korean cuisine since almost all vegetables are eaten in this fashion; vegetables are parboiled to retain crispness and colour then are dressed with a sauce of soy, sesame seed oil, prepared sesame seed flavouring, vinegar and sugar: **Cho na** mixed vegetables; **keen kong** beans; **sang chu** lettuce.

Naig kook Cucumber slices marinated in vinegar, sugar and sesame seed oil and chillis and served cold in chicken broth.

Neng myun Fine noodles in cold broth garnished with marinated beef strips, cucumber slices, hardboiled egg slices and sliced pears with mustard and vinegar sauce.

Oi jim Cucumbers filled with marinated minced meat, fried.

Oi kook Cucumber soup with marinated beef slices and eggs.

Ojingo pokum Fresh squid stir-fried with vegetables and spiced with hot chilli peppers, garlic, onion and soy.

Ok vhonh juhn Round onion wedges rolled in flour, dipped in egg and fried.

Oo duhl purn yuk Tongue boiled in soy-flavoured broth served with vinegar and soy sauce.

Oo sul kui Tongue slices marinated in soy, garlic, sugar, onion and sesame seed, broiled or fried.

Oo yuk puen yuk Beef or pork boiled in soy-flavoured broth and served with vinegar and soy sauce.

Oo yuk sahn juhk Beef strips marinated in soy, onion, garlic, sugar and sesame seed flavouring, skewered, sprinkled with sesame seeds, and fried.

Pah kook Green onion soup with beef strips and egg drop.

Pah sahn juhk Beef strips and green onions skewered alternately, coated in flour dipped in egg and fried; served sliced in small squares with vinegar and soy sauce.

Paht jook Gruel of rice and red beans.

Paj hoo kook Cabbage soup flavoured with marinated beef strips served with an egg stirred into it.

Palm pahb Rice cooked with chestnuts.

Pi bium pahb A one-dish meal of white rice tossed with marinated beef strips, parboiled bean sprouts, carrots, celery and cucumbers flavoured with soy, garlic, sesame seeds and decorated with pears and egg omelette strips.

Pori pahb Rice cooked with barley.

Puh sul kook Mushroom soup flavoured with marinated beef strips, garlic, onions and sesame seeds.

Pyun su Thin flour dumplings filled with minced chicken, mushrooms, cucumber, carrot and pine nuts served in chicken broth garnished with egg omelette strips.

Sang cha Drink made of fresh ginger root and spices.

Sang juhn kwa Candied fresh ginger.

Sang newl Peeled, raw chestnuts immersed in sweetened water.

Sang si jo rim Boned fish pieces highly spiced with soy, peppers, garlic, eaten in small amounts as a condiment.

Sang suhn jim Boned fish fillets layered with chopped beef, bamboo shoots, celery, mushrooms and carrots sprinkled with green onions, chilli pepper, candied ginger and soy, slow-simmered and served garnished with egg omelette strips.

Sang suhn jo rim Fish slices simmered in soy, ginger, pepper and garlic.

Sang suhn juhn Boned fish slices coated in flour, dipped in egg and fried.

Sang suhn kook Fish soup flavoured with beef strips, soy and garlic served with bean sprouts and turnip slices.

Sangchee na mool Lettuce salad dressed with soy, sesame seeds and chilli flecks.

Sao o juhn Shrimp rolled in flour, dipped in egg and fried.

Seekumchee juhn Skewered spinach plants coated in flour, dipped in egg and fried.

Seekumchee na mool Spinach cooked with chopped beef, onion, garlic, chilli pepper and soy sauce.

Shikumchee Parboiled spinach salad dressed with soy, garlic, sugar and sesame seed oil.

Shikumchee taeng jang kook Soup of beef stock with spinach, bean curd and squid flavoured with garlic and soy bean paste.

Sin sul lo The name of a metal bowl with a slim stem in the centre which holds burning charcoal; a selection of foods is brought to the table – marinated beef strips, fried liver, mushrooms, parboiled turnip slices, spinach, nuts – the food is layered in the sin sul lo and allowed to cook at the table.

Solong tang Wheat noodles in beef broth flavoured with ginger, soy and garlic garnished with beef strips and egg omelette.

Song i jim Mushroom slices sandwiched with flavoured minced beef, coated in flour, dipped in egg and fried.

Song i pahb Rice cooked with minced beef, mushrooms and onions, flavoured with soy, sesame seeds and garlic.

Song i pokkum Minced beef cooked with mushrooms in soy sauce.

Song i sahn juhk Marinated beef strips skewered alternately with mushroom slices, coated with flour, dipped in egg and fried.

Soong nyung A rice water drink.

Song pyun Small sweet steamed rice cakes with fillings of puréed chestnuts and red beans.

Tak kui Chicken meat squares marinated in soy, pepper and garlic, broiled or fried.

Tang kun na mool Carrot, turnip and cucumber salad dressed with vinegar and sugar.

Tang soo au Fish marinated in soy, deep-fried and served in a sweet-sour sauce combined with parboiled mushrooms, lotus roots and carrots.

Thak jim Boiled chicken pieces simmered in soy, garlic, ginger and chillis served with green peppers, carrots, and mushrooms.

Thak tuigim jang Chicken cubes in batter deep-fried served mixed with deep-fried carrots and potatoes in sweet sauce flavoured with ginger, chillis and garlic.

Wan jah juhn Flavoured minced beef cakes dipped in flour and egg, fried.

Wan ja kook Soup of beef meatballs and bean curds flavoured with onion, garlic, sesame seeds, soy, chilli peppers and pine nuts, rolled in flour, dipped in egg and fried, then combined with marinated beef cubes and mushrooms to simmer in broth, served decorated with egg omelette strips.

Yachae tweegim Diced potatoes, onion, carrot, sweet pepper and courgettes mixed in batter and fried into small cakes.

Yak kwa Small flour cakes deep-fried, soaked in sugar syrup, rolled in chopped pine nuts.

Yookehjank kook Stew of beef slices and spring onions in broth flavoured with chilli peppers, garlic and sesame seeds.

You raan Mashed, boiled chestnuts flavoured with sugar and cinnamon, formed into balls and rolled in ground pine nuts.

Yuk pyh Beef slices marinated in soy and sugar, sprinkled with chopped pine nuts and left to dry outdoors, then broiled to crispness; served cut into small squares and eaten as a condiment with rice.

Yum tong kui Beef heart slices marinated in soy, garlic, sugar and sesame seeds, broiled or fried.

Yum tong pok kum Marinated beef heart slices simmered with onions.

Useful words

Juhn A method of cooking in which meat, fish or vegetables are coated in flour, dipped in egg and fried.

Keem chee A pickle of cabbages or radishes usually very hot and spicy served as a condiment with all meals.

Kochujang Hot bean mash—ground dried chilli peppers mixed with mashed beans—used as an indispensable flavouring in most dishes.

Na mool Salad—a favourite Korean food—almost every kind of vegetable is blanched lightly and dressed with vinegar, soy and sugar.

MALAYSIA AND SINGAPORE

Agar agar dengan Agar agar (type of seaweed) reconstituted with water and sugar, mixed with egg and steamed into custard.

Achar awak Selection of mixed vegetables in season cut into strips, blanched and served with a sauce of chilli, garlic, vinegar and crushed peanuts.

Ayam golek Whole chicken simmered with tomatoes, onions, vinegar and coconut milk.

Ayam kelantan Chicken spread with a mixture of coconut milk, onions, chillis and prawn paste then barbecued.

Ayam kichup A festive dish in which chicken pieces are stir-fried in a spicy paste of lemon grass, onions, ginger, garlic and chillis then simmered in tamarind water, soy, sugar.

Babi kecap Soy-marinated pork cubes fried then simmered with mushrooms in spicy ginger and soy sauce.

Boeboe ayam Chicken and rice soup flavoured with chillis.

Bola bola tahu Bean curd and shrimp balls served in a sweet-sour sauce with tomatoes and snow peas garnished with onion rings and coriander.

Gado gado Mixed blanched vegetables in season served with ground peanuts, garlic and chilli sauce garnished with hardboiled eggs, fried onion rings and lettuce; this is a basic vegetable dish served throughout Indonesia, Malaysia and Singapore.

Gerinting udang Shrimps marinated in tamarind water, garlic and soy, coated with egg-rice flour batter and deep-fried.

Goreng sotong Squid marinated in sauce of tamarind water, ginger, garlic and soy, deep-fried.

Gulai daging lembu Chicken pieces simmered in curry sauce, chillis and coconut milk.

Gulai ikan Basic fish curry – the sauce typical of south-east Asia in the use of coconut milk as a base and use of tamarind water, lemon grass and fresh chillis as flavouring agents.

Gulai pakis Young fern heads or fiddleheads simmered in sauce of Malaysian curry flavoured with tamarind water and mint leaves.

Gulai tumis Fish cutlets simmered in spicy curry sauce.

Ikan asam Fish fillets simmered in sauce of ground almonds, ginger, chillis and lemon juice.

Ikan berinti Whole boned fish stuffed with a mixture of minced shrimps, water chestnuts, beef, ginger and spices, coated in flour and deep-fried, served with sauce of tomatoes and soy.

Jarp we mun yue Whole fish stewed in chilli, onion, soy and sugar sauce with shredded pork, salt cabbage and mushrooms.

Jarp yun yuk Cubes of beef marinated in sugar and tamarind water, rolled in a spicy nut, prawn paste and ginger mixture then simmered in coconut milk.

Jow ho yay Oysters rolled in egg and breadcrumbs and deep-fried.

Kachang bendi goreng rumpah Vegetables in season stir-fried in sauce of ground nuts, chillis and onions served with prawns.

Kambing korma Lamb cubes marinated in paste of garlic and shallots, stir-fried with other spices, then simmered in tamarind water.

Kelapa sayur Chopped vegetables simmered in spicy coconut milk.

Kepiting pedas Crabs fried with lemon juice, served with sauce of chillis, onions, garlic, tomatoes and soy.

Krupuk Shrimp crackers eaten as an appetiser or with meals as a side dish.

Kue dadar Pancakes filled with grated coconut flavoured with cloves and cinnamon simmered in brown sugar liquid.

Laksa asam Noodles in sour fish soup flavoured with tamarind water.

Laksa lemak Elaborate soup of chicken meat, shrimps, tofu, bean sprouts and vermicelli flavoured with spices and sambal badjak (chilli and onion paste).

Martabak Quick-fried envelopes of thin dough stuffed with minced meat and spices—a popular snack food.

Masak lemak Cabbage cooked in coconut milk and prawn paste.

Mee goreng Fried noodles served with shredded chicken, prawns and vegetables.

Moolie Fish fillets simmered in sauce of chillis, spices and coconut milk served with sliced tomatoes.

Opor Chicken pieces marinated in spice mixture, fried with coconut flakes, onions and lemon peel then simmered in coconut milk.

Otak otak Fish flakes, spices, coconut milk and eggs steamed or wrapped in small packets and grilled.

Pergedel jagung Corn fritters flavoured with chillis and garlic, with prawns eaten as a snack or as part of a meal with vegetables.

Pisang goreng Banana coated in rice flour fried in butter.

Popiah Paper-thin pastry filled with a mixture of vegetables, shrimps, shredded pork, chillis and garlic, fried.

Rempah rempah Fritters of prawns and bean sprouts flavoured with garlic, onions and spices, deep-fried.

Rempeyek kacang Peanut fritters flavoured with garlic and coriander eaten as a snack food or as an appetiser.

Rujak Fresh fruits dressed with coconut milk and chilli powder.

Sambal As in Indonesia, hot chilli-based sauces are an omni-present condiment on the Malaysian-Singapore table.

Sambal babi Cubes of belly pork simmered in broth of ginger, garlic, shrimp paste, chillis, lemon and coconut milk.

Sambal blachan The most common Malaysian side dish—a condiment of ground chillis and shrimp paste.

Sambal goreng ikan bilis Dried whitefish deep-fried, then flaked and mixed with chillis and spices.

Sambal ikan Whole fish coated in flour and deep-fried then simmered in spices, chillis and coconut milk.

Sambal sotong Squid stir-fried in paste of chillis and spices.

Sambal tumis Side dish of chillis, prawns, brown sugar and tamarind water ground to a paste and fried.

Sarikauga Coconut custard.

Sate As in Indonesia, meat marinated in a peppery soy-based sauce, skewered and grilled over charcoal fire, is popular throughout Malaysia and Singapore.

Sate ayam Chicken breast cubes marinated in sauce and skewered to cook over charcoal fire.

Sate babi Pork cubes marinated in honey-soy sauce, skewered and grilled.

Sate kambing Lamb cubes marinated in garlic, ginger and soy, skewered and grilled.

Sayur lemak Stew of mixed vegetables in season flavoured with spices and chillis cooked in beef broth.

Sayur lotay Selection of vegetables in season simmered in coconut milk flavoured with chillis, garlic, onions and sugar.

Sookmuytont Chicken broth with chicken meat and corn.

Soto ayam Spiced chicken soup.

Teloh dardeh Omelette of onions and chillis.

Udang ubi Prawns cooked in spicy sauce with potatoes.

Useful words

Agar agar Dried seaweed used as flavouring agent and to thicken sauces.

Assam Acid-flavoured fruit (tamarind) essential to many sauces.

Balachan Pungent shrimp paste used to flavour many dishes.

Belimbing wuluh Common fruit of south-east Asia, sour in taste.

Buah keras Pale yellow nuts commonly used as a flavouring ingredient in many south-east Asian dishes.

Bumbu Term for any mixture of ingredients that gives a strong flavour to a dish; can refer to the dry ingredients or to the sauces derived from them.

Cabe rawit Small, very hot chillis—red, green or white in colour.

Ebi Tiny, uncooked shrimps used as a flavouring agent.

Kecap Soy sauce—darker and sweeter than Chinese variety.

THE PHILIPPINES

Adobo A cooking style rather than a dish so the ingredients vary from cook to cook and place to place but it is usually a combination of pork and chicken pieces marinated in a mixture of garlic, bay leaves, onion, vinegar and soy sauce, boiled in water until the meat is tender, then fried briskly over high heat until they are coated with the cooking liquid but almost dry.

Adobo manok batangas Chicken pieces marinated in crushed garlic, vinegar and peppercorns, simmered in coconut milk with chapote (a squash vegetable).

Adobong manok at baboy A combination of boneless pork cut into cubes and chicken pieces simmered in vinegar, garlic and pepper, fried then simmered again in coconut milk, served with pineapple and tomatoes.

Adobong musit Squid marinated in vinegar, garlic and soy cooked with onions and tomatoes in the marinade liquid.

Adobong sugpo Marinated prawns fried in butter.

Asado a manok Chicken rubbed with flavouring mixture of soy vinegar and sugar, roasted over high flame for crispy skin.

Bagoong A thick paste made from fermented fish or shrimps and salt for use as a relish or flavouring agent.

Balut Duck egg with partially developed embryo considered a delicacy, served hardboiled.

Besugo Whole fish coated with bagoong (fish paste), roasted.

Bibingka Coconut cake.

Bibingka kamateng kahoy Cassava and coconut cake.

Bokayong niog Coconut candy.

Bombones de arroz Rice fritters of eggs, sugar, vanilla and coconut, deep-fried, coated in powder sugar and eaten between meals as a snack rather than as a dessert.

Camatis ken sili Tomato and green pepper casserole.

Camotig guinet taan Sweet potatoes boiled in coconut milk.

Chorizo Sausage.

Digo ti manok Chicken soup.

Dilis Dried anchovies.

Ensaimada Sugary coiled buns.

Escabeche Whole red snapper, sea bass or other white fish coated in batter, deep-fried then served with stir-fried onions and green peppers in a slightly thickened sauce of vinegar, sugar and bagoong; the most popular method of preparing fish in the Philippines.

Escabetseng aphap Whole sea bass deep-fried and served in a sweet-sour sauce flavoured with peppers, garlic and ginger.

Ginatan Fruits and vegetables such as bananas, breadfruit, taro, potatoes and yams simmered in coconut cream, sugar and lime juice.

Halo halo Liquid dessert of coconut milk and sugar served iced.

Inona a ican Marinated fish fillets tied into bundles of banana leaves and steamed.

Isdang may salsang agri-dulce Whole fish coated in batter, deep-fried and served in a sweet-sour sauce reminiscent of Chinese sweet-sour fish.

Kari kari Oxtail stew cooked with onion, garlic and ginger in slightly thickened sauce flavoured with soy, vinegar and bagoong.

Lechon Roast suckling pig.

Linengta a carabasa Boiled squash served with vinegary sauce.

Linengta a maize Boiled green corn.

Litsong baboy Suckling pig stuffed with prunes, roasted over coals or in oven and served with liver sauce (ground liver, onion, garlic, vinegar and brown sugar).

Lumpia Thin pancakes filled with lettuce and cooked vegetables.

Lumpia sariwa Thin flour skins filled with elaborate mixture of stir-fried onions, garlic, pork, ham, prawns, beans, shredded carrots, diced potatoes, cabbage, cooked until tender but crisp then deep-fried; a favourite variation is to wrap the filling in lettuce leaves without deep-frying – served with sauce of chicken stock, soy, brown sugar, garlic and bagoong.

Mongo Shrimp with mung beans, tomatoes and garlic served with braised spinach and fish sauce.

Morcon Beef sheet spread with mixture of ham, hardboiled eggs, raisins, olives and onion simmered in broth of tomatoes, onion and vinegar, served with sauce of thickened cooking liquid.

Napalet a chocolate Thick chocolate drink.

Paksiw Whole fish simmered with bitter melon, aubergine, ginger and chillis in a vinegary broth.

Paksiw na litson Stew of pork, liver sauce, vinegar, soy and garlic.

Pan de sal Small, salted crisp rolls.

Pansit gisado Fried noodles garnished with shrimps, chicken, ham or pork and shredded cabbage, flavoured with garlic, soy, bagoong and onion.

Pata Crisp roast pork knuckles.

Pipino at camates Cucumber and tomato salad.

Puto Sweet steamed rice cake.

Quesa de bola Cheese.

Rebosadong hipon Shrimp and ham fritters.

Rellenong alimango Crab shells stuffed with crab meat and scallions and fried.

Rellenong hipon Large shrimps stuffed with mixture of minced pork, green onions, wrapped in egg roll skins and deep-fried.

Rellenong manok Boned whole chicken marinated in soy, stuffed with ground veal, pork, Chinese ham, chorizo (sausage), eggs, green olives, pimento, sweet pickles and raisins, steamed then roasted.

Sampalok Sour green tamarinds – an acidy flavouring agent.
Sawsawang kamatis Tomato salad dressed with scallion, minced green mango, lime juice and ginger.
Sawsawang sila Chili-flavoured vinegar.
Sinampalukan Thick sour soup of tamarind leaves, fish or chicken and vegetables.
Sinangag Rice cooked with pork fat and garlic.
Sinigang Soup with seafood, vegetables and sour fruits.
Sinigang na isda Stew of fresh fish, aubergines, banana blossoms, carrots, onions, radishes, sweet peppers and tomatoes flavoured with bagoong, soy, garlic and tamarind water.
Sotanghon Chicken pieces marinated in vinegar, crushed garlic and bagoong cooked with transparent noodles.
Suman Little elongated cakes made of glutinous rice flour wrapped in palm leaves and steamed.

Tapa Marinated beef or pork slices dried and quick-fried.
Tapang baka Lean slices of beef cured in salt and deep-fried.
Tinono a camotig Baked yams.

Ukoy Little pancakes filled with chopped shrimps, grated sweet potatoes and pumpkin.

Useful words

Bagoong Paste of fermented fish or shrimp, the universal flavouring agent of the Philippines.
Bunga Fruit.
Cha Tea.
Cape Coffee.
Isda Fish.
Kanin Rice.
Karne Meat.
Miti Wide egg noodles.
Patis Fish sauce of salted anchovies.
Tinapay Bread.

THAILAND

Bamee nahm Egg noodles in chicken broth garnished with chopped chicken, beef, seafood or Chinese roast pork flavoured with coriander, green onion, celery, served with chillis, fish sauce and pickled peppers.

Beeyak cahmpoht Tender corn kernels simmered in coconut milk then thickened with flaked coconut.

Bet yahng Duck marinated in sauce of honey, soy, vinegar, garlic, mashed brown beans and chilli powder, then spit-roasted; when outer layer is cooked, skin is removed and eaten separately with rice and oyster sauce – the partially cooked flesh is then stir-fried with celery, bean sprouts and simmered with oyster sauce, chicken broth and sugar and served with rice as a second course.

Bobpeeuh Minced chicken, pork, onion, mushroom and vermicelli noodles wrapped in delicate egg skins and deep-fried.

Boo paht tawn ga tiem Crab stir-fried with savoury sauce of garlic, brown beans, soy bean condiment, fish sauce and leeks.

Choo chee Whole fish deep-fried and served covered with sauce of curry paste, coconut cream and fish sauce garnished with coriander sprigs.

Cow neeoh mimawn Rice pudding made with sugar and coconut cream, served with mango slices.

Cow paht Fried rice with beef, pork and chicken pieces flavoured with green chillis and fish sauce served with tomatoes and beaten eggs.

Cow tawm paht Glutinous rice cooked in coconut cream, shaped into dumplings filled with fruit or Chinese sweet red bean paste and steamed.

Dawm fang mahm Spare-ribs and winter melon soup flavoured with fish sauce.

Dow hoo tawt ham jim Tofu cubes deep-fried and served with sauce of ground peanuts, vinegar and chillis.

Fan taeng Marrow stuffed with minced pork flavoured with fish sauce and garlic, steamed and served surrounded by prawns and crab meat.

Foi tawng krob Beaten egg yolks drizzled into sugar syrup to form golden strands.

Fuk tawng sy ky Pumpkin and egg omelette flavoured with fish paste.

Gadook moo paht gatiem plik ty Spare-ribs marinated in garlic, chillis and fish sauce then stir-fried with onion and tomatoes.

Gai paht Chicken breast cubes stir-fried with miniature corn cobs, straw mushrooms, chilli peppers and garlic then simmered in chicken broth, oyster sauce, fish sauce, soy, served topped with toasted cashew nuts.

Gai paht king Boned chicken shreds stir-fried with ginger (treated as a vegetable), wood fungus and garlic then simmered with fish sauce, soy and chilli peppers.

Gai tawm ka Chicken pieces fried then simmered in sauce of chilli peppers, fish paste, coconut cream and galingale (root similar to ginger).

Gai yang Spiced fresh chicken, barbecued to a rich brown colour.

Gang ba Fillets of fish stir-fried with vegetables and fish sauce.

Gang chood wun sen Minced pork balls simmered in chicken broth with addition of Chinese cabbage and vermicelli noodles, flavoured with fish sauce.

Gang karee Thai curry of chillis, onions, coriander, cumin, turmeric and lemon grass, ground to a paste.

Gang keal wan goong Shrimps, green peas and citrus leaves simmered in curry paste, coconut cream, chilli peppers and fish paste.

Gang keal wan hoouh Beef cubes in curry sauce made green with addition of chopped spinach.

Gang mus sa mun Beef cubes simmered in curry paste, coconut cream, fish sauce and lime juice with potatoes and peanuts.

Gang pet gai Chicken pieces and bamboo shoots simmered in sauce of coconut cream, chillis, fish sauce and sugar.

Gang sawm Fish fillets boiled, flaked and mixed with curry paste in sweet-sour sauce, then simmered with addition of vegetables such as bamboo shoots, green beans, cabbages or broccoli.

Gang tom yam Clear soup garnished with prawns, chicken meat and fish served in a charcoal heated brazier.

Goong yai Elaborate dish of lobster halves laid on bed of pork strips and bean thread noodles with sauce of soy, fish sauce, ginger, rice wine, garlic and crushed peppercorns poured over the dish and baked.

Gwayteeo niuh Soup of beef ribs and vermicelli noodles highly spiced with fish sauce, chillis, vinegar and herbs.

Haw moke Chopped fish steamed on a bed of fresh vegetables.

Ho mok Flaked fish, grated coconut, leeks, coconut cream, eggs and curry paste, wrapped in banana leaves and steamed.

Hoi paht by holapa Clams in the shell stir-fried with chillis, garlic, basil, fish sauce and soy.

Jang Pork chops marinated in soy, chilli and coriander paste, grilled over charcoal fire.

Kaeng chud Coconut milk broth flavoured with paste of onions, garlic, fish sauce, soy and chilli served with chopped prawns and lemon peel.

Kaeng chud kai kabhed Boiled, boned chicken served in cooking broth with Chinese mushrooms, fish sauce, soy and garlic.

Kaeng chud pla Flaked fish formed into balls with coriander, garlic and pepper, simmered in fish broth with mushrooms, pork strips and bean curds and flavoured with fish sauce and spring onions.

Kaeng chud saku Soup of chicken stock, minced pork, flaked crab meat and Chinese cabbage thickened with tapioca.

Kaeng ho mai Spare-ribs stir-fried with spices and chillis then simmered in chicken broth with bamboo shoots.

Kaeng masaman Curry of chicken or beef – the meat is first simmered in coconut milk then mixed with a spicy but mild curry sauce based on tamarind water; peanuts are added along with fish sauce in the last stage of cooking.

Kaeng phet kai Chicken meat simmered in coconut milk flavoured with hot curry paste and fish sauce served with aubergines.

Kaeng phet nua Beef simmered in coconut milk flavoured with hot curry paste and fish sauce.

Kaeng tom yam Leg of pork stuffed with ground pork flavoured with garlic, coriander and soy, deep-fried then simmered in chicken broth with lemon slices and chillis.

Kai look koei Hardboiled eggs fried until crisp and warmed in tamarind water and sugar.

Kai panang Chicken breast cubes simmered in coconut cream flavoured with curry paste.

Kai tod Chicken coated with a paste of garlic, coriander, pepper and fish sauce, fried.

Kai tod karb kratiem Chicken breasts marinated in garlic, soy, sugar and sesame seed oil, stir-fried.

Kai tom kha Chicken pieces simmered in coconut milk flavoured with chillis, lemon peel and soy sauce.

Kai tord Chicken pieces marinated in garlic, chilli pepper and coriander root paste and deep-fried.

Kai yad sai Egg skins filled with minced pork mixture and deep-fried.

Kam koong Boiled prawns served with sauce of coconut milk in which are cooked peanuts, apples and green peppers.

Kang ron Elaborate soup of minced pork balls, prawns, dried squid, dried mushrooms and vermicelli noodles.

Kanome A wide variety of jellied sweets with an agar agar, coconut cream and sugar base.

Kanome puak goowum Candy of taro root cooked in coconut and sugar syrup.

Kao lao luk chin Clear soup with meatballs and bean sprouts.

Kao pot ping Corn ears dipped in coconut milk and roasted.

Kao thung Deep-fried dried rice sheets – a snack food.

Kao tom kai Minced chicken balls lightly flavoured with soy, cooked in chicken broth with soft-boiled rice.

Kayanthi hmat Aubergines stuffed with mixture of chopped prawns, chicken, garlic and onions seasoned with chilli, baked.

Khai cheow Plain omelette.

Khan om kluk Rice flour pancakes topped with sugar, coconut flakes and cream.

Kia chem pria wan Chicken in sweet and spicy sauce with onions, tomatoes, green peppers and cucumbers.

Kow neo sang kaya Custard of eggs and coconut cream served with sweet glutinous rice mixed with coconut cream, steamed.

Kow neo tua dom Glutinous rice, black beans and sugar stuffed into hollow bamboo sticks and cooked over charcoal fire.

Kow tom kai Rice porridge made with chicken breasts and pork flavoured with fish sauce, usually taken at breakfast.

Ky yaht sy Ground pork flavoured with fish sauce, stir-fried with green peas and used as filling for egg skins.

Lahp isan Sautéed minced beef with fish sauce.

Luk nua Meat cakes of minced pork, beef, garlic, fish sauce and eggs coated with flour and fried.

Mah ho Minced pork stir-fried with peanuts and onions, served on pineapple slices or stuffed into orange shells.

Maled khanun Crushed mung beans cooked in coconut cream, formed into balls and simmered in sugar syrup.

Mee krob Rice vermicelli deep-fried into puffs and garnished with shrimps and pork flavoured with fish sauce, tomato paste, ginger and coriander.

Miang kai krathong krorp Cups made of flour and coconut milk which are filled with a mixture of minced chicken, peanuts, ginger, onion and garlic — a cocktail food.

Moh thong leung Thick broth of tripe, beef and bamboo shoots cooked in beef broth — named after the pot in which the food is cooked.

Mok si kao Cake of rice flour, grated coconut and bananas.

Moo paht gatiem plik ty Pork cubes marinated in sauce of coriander, garlic and fish sauce stir-fried with onion and tomatoes.

Moo tod Minced pork flavoured with fish sauce, garlic and coriander root formed into balls and deep-fried.

Mus sa mun Thai-style curry paste of chilli peppers, garlic, lemon grass, onion, sugar, cumin and cardamom.

Nam Sour-flavoured pork sausage usually eaten raw.

Nam prik Usually refers to the universal Thai dish of vegetable selection, either raw or boiled or deep-fried in batter, always accompanied by the nam prik sauce after which it is named — the sauce is a combination of minced prawns, chillis, lime juice, garlic and fish sauce.

Nam prik deng chiengmai Sauce of chillis, onion, garlic and salted fish pounded into a paste.

Nam prik deng thai Hot sauce with boiled vegetables — any variety in season — lightly boiled in coconut milk.

Nam prik gapee Vegetables in season served with a nam prik sauce flavoured with dried shrimp paste (gapee).

Nam prik nam ya A sweetish curry with flaked fish served over boiled vermicelli.

Nam prik ong Minced pork stir-fried with nam prik sauce and simmered in tomatoes.

Nam prik pak Raw vegetables with hot sauce — a spectrum of taste and colour with such as roots, leaves, tubers, flowers.

Nam prik pao Hot sauce in which chillis, onions and garlic are roasted in ashes before being pounded into paste.

Noouh gap toouh Beef simmered in coconut milk, then reheated with paste of ground peanuts, chilli, tamarind water and braised spinach.

Nua nam toak Grilled beef dressed with mashed onions and chillis served surrounded by a ring of vegetables in season.

Nua pad prik Beef cubes stir-fried with chillis, garlic and coriander.

Nua tang Minced pork and prawns simmered in coconut milk flavoured with sugar and chilli peppers.

Pad horapa kub nua Beef stir-fried with chillis, onions, garlic and horapa leaves (similar to basil).

Pad thua ngork Stir-fried bean sprouts, prawns and pork flavoured with fish sauce and garlic.

Paht bleeoh wan Pork cubes stir-fried with chillis and onions, simmered in sweet-sour sauce with pineapples and tomatoes.

Paht by kaprow Squid stir-fried with mint, chillis, soy and fish sauce.

Paht pahk Selection of vegetables stir-fried and seasoned lightly with fish sauce or chilli, a usual accompaniment to curry.

Paht pahk nahm mahn hoi Collard greens stir-fried with oyster sauce.

Paht thai The national noodle dish – rice noodles garnished with ground peanuts, shrimps, radishes, bean curds, fish sauce, chillis, leeks and egg strips.

Paht toouh ngawk hap dow hoo Bean sprouts and bean curds stir-fried with fish sauce and soy.

Ped yang Duck marinated with five-spice powder, pepper, garlic and soy, roasted.

Peek kai namdang Fried chicken wings in a sweet-sour sauce.

Pla chien Fried fish steamed in sharp chilli and ginger sauce.

Pla prio wan Whole fish coated with flour and deep-fried served in sweet-sour sauce.

Poh tack Seafood and mushrooms simmered in tamarind water.

Pra ram long song Beef fried with garlic and onions then simmered with vegetables.

Prikchee sy moo Mild green chillis stuffed with flaked fish or minced pork, baked or steamed.

Pu ja Crab meat mixed with minced pork, mushrooms and garlic, stuffed into crab shells and deep-fried.

Sakoo Tapioca cooked in coconut cream with corn kernels and water chestnuts.

Saku sai mooh Sago (starchy palm plant) stuffed with minced pork, chopped peanut, sugar and onion mixture.

Sawm tahm Thai-style coleslaw of papaya, green beans, chopped peanuts, shrimps, chillis, sugar and fish sauce.

Som tum Salad of cabbage, carrots, crushed peanuts, dressed with fish sauce, garlic, sugar and lime juice.

Tao chiew lon Dip of mashed beans, prawns and chillis in coconut cream served with a selection of vegetables.

Tawm yahm Chicken broth with chicken or shrimp meat and mushrooms, flavoured with coconut cream, chillis and lemon juice.

Tawt mon bla Curried fish cakes deep-fried and served with a sauce of peanuts, cucumber and chilli powder.

Tod mun pla Flaked fish, garlic and chillis formed into balls and deep-fried, served with sliced cucumbers.

Tom yam kung Prawns, crayfish or lobster simmered in broth flavoured with lemon grass, chillis, nam prik pao (prepared hot sauce) and lime leaves.

Tom yum kung lae pla muk Shrimp and squid soup flavoured with chillis and garlic.

Tord mun jung Minced prawns mixed with spices and chillis, shaped into balls, rolled in breadcrumbs and deep-fried.

Yam Literally, to mix with the hand; salads of cooked or raw vegetables served with a hot sauce (nam prik).

Yam chomphu Salad of tart fruit – pineapple, green mangoes, sour apples – pork strips and prawns served with lemon juice, sugar and fish sauce.

Yam taeng Crisp vegetables – cucumbers, radishes, water chestnuts, lettuce – served with a sweet-sour sauce flavoured with fish sauce.

Yam yai Elaborate salad of prawns, pork strips, chicken breast strips, vermicelli, cucumbers, bean sprouts, mushrooms and other vegetables served with a hot sauce and garnished with hardboiled eggs, coriander and chillis.

Useful words

Asam Tamarind – an acid-flavoured fruit resembling a bean pod.

Horapa An herb much like sweet basil.

Kapi Pungent shrimp paste.

Kha Galingale – the root of a plant resembling ginger.

Makrut Strongly flavoured citrus fruit; peel is ground and mixed with other ingredients in curry pastes and leaves are used in soup.

Nam pla Fish sauce.

Tao chiew Salted bean flavouring.

VIETNAM

Bahn cam Balls of glutinous rice flour cakes filled with sweetened mung bean paste, rolled in sesame seeds and deep-fried.

Bahn mi chien tom Bread spread with prawn paste and deep-fried.

Bap cai nhoi tom thit Ground pork, shrimp, noodles, mushrooms, onions and fish sauce wrapped in cabbage leaves and steamed.

Bo kho Beef stew flavoured with curry paste, fish sauce and ginger, simmered with carrots.

Bo nhung dam Beef cubes cooked by diner fondue-style in a broth of vinegar, sugar and beef broth served with carrots and turnips marinated in vinegar and sugar.

Bo nuong Beef slices marinated in fish sauce, garlic and onions grilled and served with carrots and turnips marinated in vinegar and sugar and eaten with nuoc mam sauce (fish paste).

Bo sao hanh tay Beef slices marinated in fish sauce and stir-fried with onions.

Bo xao bong cai Beef cubes marinated in fish sauce, stir-fried with cauliflower.

Bo xao ca chua can Beef marinated in garlic and fish sauce, stir-fried with tomatoes and celery.

Bo xao mang Beef stir-fried with bamboo shoots flavoured with fish sauce.

Bo xao rau Beef marinated in garlic and fish sauce stir-fried with cabbage, onion, carrot and celery.

Bun bo xao Vermicelli noodles served with garnishes of marinated beef stir-fried, shredded lettuce, carrots and radishes flavoured with crushed peanuts and nuoc mam sauce.

Bun thit heo Soup of pork, tomatoes, rice vermicelli noodles served with shredded lettuce and fish sauce.

Bun thit nuong Grilled pork marinated in garlic and fish sauce served over vermicelli noodles garnished with carrots and radishes.

Ca chua nhoi thit Tomatoes stuffed with minced pork flavoured with onion and fish sauce, fried.

Ca hap Fish coated with a mixture of sliced pork, ginger, sugar, shallots and fish sauce topped with diced mushrooms and steamed.

Ca kho thom Fried fish steaks layered with pineapples and simmered with shallots.

Ca nau ca chua Fish and tomato soup flavoured with dill and fish sauce.

Ca xao chua Fish fillets fried then simmered in tomato and fish sauce broth.

Canh chua Sour fish soup flavoured with fish sauce, tamarind water and chillis with addition of tomatoes, bean sprouts and celery.

Canh ga Chicken broth garnished with chicken strips, turnips and Chinese cabbage.

Canh ga chien bo Chicken wings marinated in soy and garlic, deep-fried.

Canh tan o thit heo Chicken broth with edible chrysanthemum leaves and pork meatballs.

Canh thit ca chua trung Pork, tomato and egg soup flavoured with fish sauce.

Cari bo Beef curry with potatoes.

Cat heo xao rau Marinated pork kidneys stir-fried with carrot strips, celery and snow peas.

Cha gio Egg rolls filled with shrimp or crab and wood ears served with fish sauce and side dish of vegetables marinated in sweet-sour sauce.

Cha gio ga Egg skins filled with a mixture of vermicelli, minced chicken or pork or a combination of seafood, flavoured with garlic and fish sauce.

Che bap Creamed corn kernel soup sweetened with sugar.

Che khoai lang Sugared sweet potatoes.

Chuoi chien Fruit fritters.

Com Plain boiled rice.

Com chien Fried rice with cooked chicken, pork or shrimp and peas flavoured with fish sauce.

Cua hap trung Flaked crab meat, ground pork, mushrooms and eggs flavoured with fish sauce and steamed.

Cua nau bot bang Chicken broth thickened with tapioca and garnished with crab meat.

Cua rang muoi Stir-fried crabs flavoured with garlic.

Cua xao ca chua Crab quarters marinated in garlic and fish sauce, stir-fried with tomatoes.

Cua xao dam Stir-fried crabs in sweet-sour sauce flavoured with fish sauce.

Dia rau song Platter of raw mixed vegetables served with fish sauce.

Dua cai Pickled mustard greens.

Ga chua ngot Stir-fried chicken wings served in a sweet-sour sauce flavoured with fish sauce.

Ga hap ca Boned chicken breasts steamed with tomatoes, ginger, chillis and fish sauce.

Ga nau nam Chicken stewed with fish sauce, mushrooms, butter and tomato paste.

Ga nuong chao Chicken coated with bean curd fragments, garlic and onion brushed with mixture of tapioca flour, vinegar and honey, left to hang until dry then baked; served with lettuce leaves and watercress.

Ga tim Chicken stuffed with lotus seeds or ground almonds mixed with ground pork, mushrooms, shallots and fish sauce, steamed then simmered in cooking stock.

Ga xao dua Chicken stir-fried with fish sauce then simmered with pineapple and celery.

Ga xao hanh nhan Boned chicken stir-fried with fish sauce served in sauce with carrots and almonds.

Ga xao mien Fried chicken flavoured with fish sauce stir-fried with bean thread noodles.

Ga xao nam rom Chicken marinated in fish sauce stir-fried with mushrooms.

Ga xao sa nuoc dua Chicken pieces marinated in garlic, sugar, curry powder, chillis and fish sauce, then stir-fried with lemon grass and finally simmered in coconut milk.

Ga xao xa ot Chicken pieces marinated in lemon peel and onions stir-fried with chillis served with crushed peanuts.

Ga xe phay Salad of chicken strips, shredded cabbage and carrots, dressed with sweet-sour sauce flavoured with fish sauce and garlic.

Gan bo xao hanh   Pork liver stir-fried with onions and fish sauce.

Gan heo nuong   Pork liver and pork cubes marinated in fish sauce, garlic and shallots then skewered and grilled over charcoal fire.

Goi tom   Salad of cucumber, carrot and celery dressed with ground peanuts, fish sauce and garlic topped with prawns and chicken strips.

Goi tom thit   Boiled pork and shrimps arranged with diced carrots, radishes and cucumbers and served with sweet-sour sauce flavoured with fish sauce.

Heo kho   Chopped onion and pork sautéed in sweet sauce simmered in coconut milk.

Hoa qua tron   Fruit salad.

Hu tiu   Soup of pork broth garnished with shrimps, pork and rice noodles.

Luon sao mien   Sautéed eel with onion and vermicelli noodles.

Mang cua   Soup of crab meat and asparagus tips.

Mien ga   Chicken soup with bean thread noodles.

Moke khat pa   Fish cubes and chopped prawns mixed with chillis and fish sauce folded into individual packets and steamed.

Muc xao chua ngot   Squid stir-fried with broccoli then blended in a sweet-sour sauce flavoured with fish sauce.

Muc xao rau   Fresh squid pieces marinated in fish sauce then stir-fried with carrot strips, onions and snow peas.

Nem noung   Pork balls skewered and grilled over charcoal fire and served on a platter surrounded by cucumber strips, lettuce leaves and rice paper; pork balls are wrapped in rice paper and leaves and dipped in sauce of crushed peanuts, chillis and mashed fermented beans.

Nuoc cham   An indispensable Vietnamese sauce served with every meal: garlic, chillis, sugar, lime juice and fish sauce mashed together into a hot paste.

Oc heo chien   Pork brain omelette flavoured with fish sauce.

Oc heo hap   Pork brain mixed with egg, fish sauce, onion and shallots, steamed.

Pho   Soup of oxtails, vegetables and rice noodles flavoured with fish sauce – speciality of North Vietnam, usually eaten as a snack food in 'soup stores'.

Phoat khat   Elaborate rice dish in which rice is cooked in chicken broth and garnished with pork strips, prawns and egg strips topped with chillis.

Suon nuong   A one-dish meal; spare-ribs marinated in paste of shallots, sugar, garlic and fish sauce roasted or grilled served over a mound of rice garnished with cucumber slices.

Thit bo kho   Beef cubes stewed in broth flavoured with curry paste, ginger, fish sauce and chillis.

Thit bo nuong vi sat   Thin slices of beef usually cooked by the diner on individual burners then wrapped in rice paper with cucumber and onion slices with lime juice and fish sauce accompaniments.

Thit heo kho tieu   Pork belly marinated in fish sauce, garlic, pepper and honey, simmered until cooking broth thickens.

Thit kho nuoc dua Beef cubes marinated in fish sauce and simmered in coconut milk.

Thit kho to Pork belly simmered in broth of garlic, ginger, onions and soy sauce.

Tom kho tau Prawns stir-fried with spring onions flavoured with fish sauce and mint.

Tom nuong banh hoi Rice noodles served with topping of grilled prawns garnished with scallions, lemon slices and coriander.

Tom vien Shrimp balls flavoured with fish sauce, pork fat, garlic and shallots deep-fried, served as an appetiser or as a side dish with rice.

Tom vo vien Paste of prawns, onions and fish sauce formed into cakes and fried.

Tom xao rau Shrimps marinated in fish sauce and stir-fried, served with stir-fried cucumber strips, cabbage and ginger.

Trung chien Ground pork, fish sauce and eggs formed into cakes and fried.

Trung chien voi cua Crab omelette flavoured with chillis and onions, fried.

Vit nuong Whole duck rubbed with mixture of soy, ginger, sugar and garlic, roasted then cut into bite-size pieces and served with ginger sauce.

Vit tan Duck marinated in ginger and rice wine and stuffed with mixture of lotus seeds, prunes, mushrooms, chestnuts, ginger, shallots and peanuts and steamed.

Vit xao mang Duck soup with bamboo shoots and vermicelli.

Xoi ga Glutinous rice and mung beans served with chicken strips marinated in fish sauce and stir-fried.

Yam Salad of pork strips, cucumber and prawns dressed with mint, garlic, coriander and lemon juice.

Useful words

Asam Tamarind—an acid-flavoured fruit flavouring agent.

Banh trang Rice papers—thin, brittle crêpes used to make spring rolls or as wrappers for a variety of fillings.

Bun tau Fine transparent noodles of mung beans.

Culantro Coriander, an essential ingredient in Vietnamese cuisine.

Galingale Known as laos in Vietnam—a root plant resembling ginger root, an essential ingredient in Vietnamese cuisine.

Nuoc cham/nuoc mam Fish sauce as important as salt made of fresh anchovies which are salted and left to ferment.